I love you
Nat !

♡ Millie

PARISIAN CHIC *encore!*

French Edition
Editorial Director
Julie Rouart
Administration Manager
Delphine Montagne
Editor
Mélanie Puchault
Design
Tiphaine Bréguë
Photo Research
Andrew Hodgson

English Edition
Editorial Director
Kate Mascaro
Editor
Helen Adedotun
Translation from the French
Kate Robinson
Typesetting
Thierry Renard
Proofreading
Lindsay Porter

Production
Christelle Lemonnier
Color Separation
IGS, L'Isle-d'Espagnac
Printed in Slovakia by TBB, a. s.

Simultaneously published in French as *La Parisienne*
© Flammarion, S.A., Paris, 2019
English-language edition
© Flammarion, S.A., Paris, 2019

editions.flammarion.com

19 20 21 3 2 1

ISBN: 978-2-08-020412-7

Legal Deposit: 10/2019

PARISIAN CHIC *encore!*

A STYLE GUIDE

Ines de la Fressange
& Sophie Gachet

DRAWINGS BY Ines de la Fressange

Flammarion

preface

Who says the Parisian woman is a myth? It's been almost ten years since I wrote *Parisian Chic* and it seems that the myth, now a *New York Times* bestseller, is real. The guide needed a little makeover. Not only were many of the addresses no longer relevant, but I moved (so everything in my house changed), and my wardrobe has gained some color. Of course I'll always wear a navy blue sweater or a white shirt, but I'm trying to reinvent myself, even if Paris will always be Paris.

Contents

DRESS LIKE A *PARISIENNE*

HOW TO LOOK PARISIAN

7 guidelines

Everyone knows you don't have
to be born in Paris to dress like a Parisian.
I'm from Saint-Tropez, I have Argentinian
roots, and I grew up in Yvelines, a suburb
of Paris. But I feel incredibly Parisian!
It isn't hard to have Paris style.
Just follow these seven guidelines.

Discreet chic

You'll never see a real Parisian dripping with
flashy jewelry, wearing a fur coat and clothes
plastered in logos. A real Parisian isn't friends with
people who say, "You wear such expensive clothes.
How wonderful!," but rather, "Have you read Simone
de Beauvoir? I love her!" These aren't really the same
kind of people.

2

Ignore trends

It's not the Parisian's style to follow the herd. Just because the "dominatrix" look ruled the catwalks doesn't mean you should go out in a shredded leather dress. The Parisian thinks about her personal look and doesn't incorporate a trend without asking herself: "Is this my style?" Nor is she the type to spend a month's wages on a bag declared "essential" by fashionistas. For one, she might not have the means, and she just isn't a follower anyway.

3

Out with the total look

The runway is the only appropriate place for the total look. A few unimaginative fashion magazines might turn their pages into a brand catalog by copy-pasting from the latest fashion shows. But there's nothing creative about that. The Parisian doesn't allow herself to be dictated to. She mixes brands, regardless of price—chic is a combination of luxury and affordability. For example: she effortlessly pairs a luxury bag she'll have all her life with worn jeans, a white T-shirt, and sneakers.

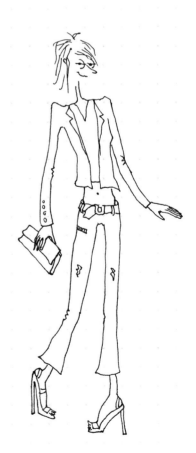

4

Be comfortable in your skin

You won't find a Parisian fussing with a plunging neckline, painful shoes, or a short skirt. Fashion pros will tell you: "The secret to style is feeling good in your clothes." If you're wearing a sweater that's too tight for you or trousers that are too snug, go change! Her motto: never be a fashion victim.

5

Create your own vintage collection

Although she regularly adds new pieces to her wardrobe, the Parisian also buys timeless clothes that she can keep for years without anyone realizing it, so skilled is she at mixing them up. She wears clothes for several seasons, stores them away, then brings them out again. "Oh this jacket? I've had it for ages."

Don't be afraid of bad taste

6

Don't bow down to fashion diktats! Even the ones in this book. If you learn one thing from this guide— which will give you plenty of good ideas—it's that good taste is the one you decide to create. Yves Saint Laurent himself made bad taste fashionable when he combined black and navy blue.

7

Be the "buyer" for your own wardrobe

A true fashion hunter, the Parisian loves finding new brands and boutiques that no one knows about. She's in seventh heaven when she discovers an independent label that is under the radar. She can't help but scout around. She loves nothing more than browsing and selecting the best from different places, whether it's a cashmere sweater by French supermarket Monoprix, Levi's jeans, or an Yves Saint Laurent suit. She operates as if she is a purchaser for a department store and doesn't blindly take advice from fashion magazines (she reads this guide instead ;-)).

LOOK BOOK

When you hear someone say "she has style,"
you might think that woman knows a secret
to being better dressed than everyone else.
You may wonder how to uncover her secret.
Ever since my days as a young model,
I've been told I have style. Maybe, but honestly,
it's not rocket science, and if you look at my closet
(pages 72–79), you'll quickly see that it all comes
down to knowing how to mix things up.
Everyone can be Parisian!
Here's the breakdown of a few very
simple looks to copy.

Parisian elegance

A black pant suit

+

A white tank top

+

A bag with personality

+

Sneakers

→ *a black pant suit,* an eternally appropriate outfit.

→ *a white tank top,* for a hint of "color."

→ *a bag with personality.* (When the outfit is simple, the accessory can stand out.)

→ *Sporty sneakers.* The contrast with the chic suit creates modern elegance.

Go for gold

A close-fitting beige turtleneck sweater

+

Bronze ⅞ cropped pants

A patent leather bag

+

Patent leather heels

> A close-fitting beige turtleneck sweater softens this look.
> Bronze ⅞ cropped pants can be worn during the day.
> A patent leather bag for contrast. And also because it transitions easily from workday to evening.
> Patent leather heels for a hint of glamour.

Pastel passion

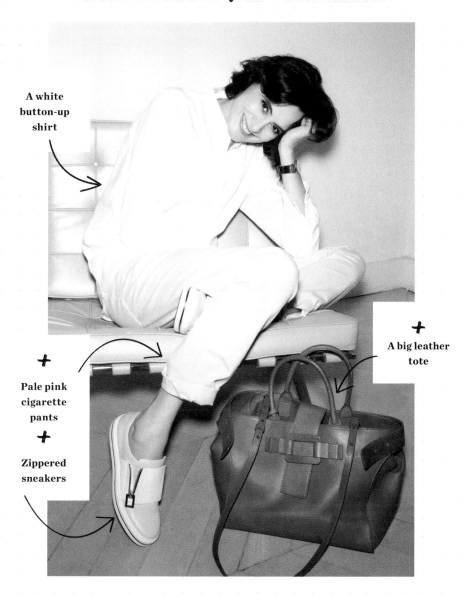

A white button-up shirt

A big leather tote

Pale pink cigarette pants

+

Zippered sneakers

→ *A white button-up shirt,* with a slightly masculine look.
→ *Pale pink cigarette pants* for a sweet, airy touch.
→ *Zippered sneakers* are sporty but very chic.
→ *A big leather tote* to round out the soft, natural look.
  (A black purse would have a different effect.)

Sophisticated denim

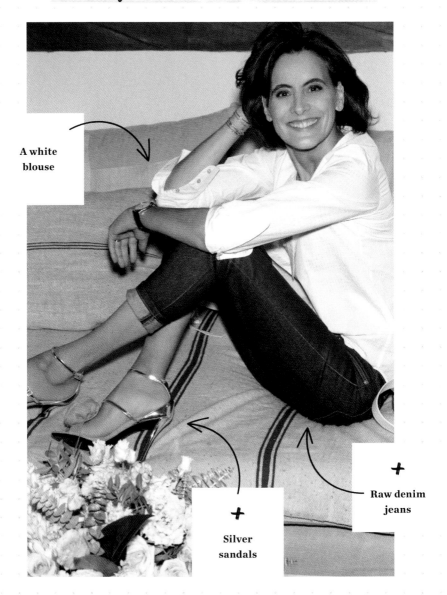

A white blouse

Raw denim jeans

Silver sandals

→ *Raw denim jeans* with cuffs. A basic that deserves good company. You can also forgo the cuffs, but it's less sophisticated.

→ *A white blouse,* also basic and raw denim's perfect match. Rolling-up the sleeves or leaving them carelessly unbuttoned is essential.

→ *Silver sandals.* An important detail that takes the look from basic to sophisticated and from day to evening.

Pattern party

A plaid coat

+

A leopard-print bag

+

White trousers

+

Grey boots

→ *a plaid coat*, now a classic in the Parisian's wardrobe.

→ *a leopard-print bag*. You've always been told not to mix wildly different patterns, but actually it adds oomph to the outfit.

→ *White trousers*. Necessary if you don't want to look like a circus runaway.

→ *Grey boots*, a plain detail that makes the outfit almost understated.

Chic but not too chic

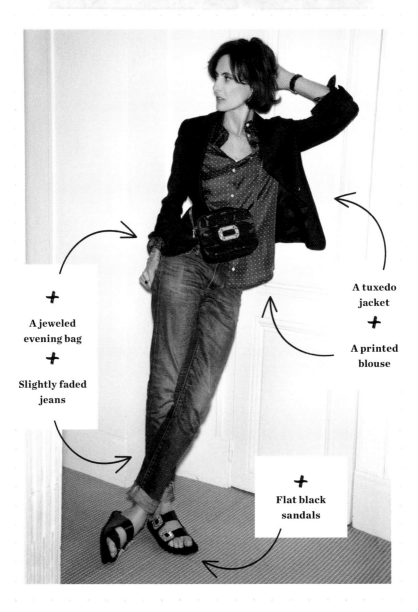

A jeweled evening bag

+

Slightly faded jeans

A tuxedo jacket

+

A printed blouse

+

Flat black sandals

→ *A tuxedo jacket,* essential for a hint of "elegance."

→ A close-fitting *printed blouse.*

→ *Slightly faded jeans,* straight-leg and cuffed.

→ *Flat black sandals* with rhinestones provide a little sparkle if you plan on going out after work.

→ *A jeweled evening bag.* Wear it across your body for a cool look (otherwise it's too fussy).

Parisian ethnic

An Indian-inspired blouse

+

Loose, printed pants

+

Ornamented flip-flops

→ *An Indian-inspired blouse* in pale pink with pinstripes is perfect for a hot day in the capital.

→ *Loose, printed pants in deep burgundy,* which goes well with pastel pink.

→ *Decorative flip-flops with rhinestones* keep the look from being too predictable.

Style questions

The killer detail

Can I wear a peacoat in the evening?

Yes, if you wear it closed over a shirt buttoned to the neck, with those famous ⅞ cropped pants and patent leather boots with gold heels to prove that you didn't come to hoist the sails. A little evening bag worn across the body clinches the soirée look.

How do you wear all white?

Choose an immaculate suit and a matching shirt. Add a few rhinestones to the bag. The same goes for the sandals. And if you want to get married in that, you can!

The killer detail

The killer detail

How do you get away with wearing plaid?

To counteract the serious (or clownish) side of a plaid pant suit, pair it with a plain sweater, white sneakers, and a straw bag. It's important to play down the all-business aspect.

How do you wear an all-fuchsia look?

This works in satin: a blouse and trousers with matching sandals. But the bag should stand out. White is a good option. Red could also break things up.

The killer detail

EASY STYLE TIPS

Sometimes you don't need much to achieve true effortless style. What does it take? Self-confidence … and a smile! (Everything's easier when you smile.) Here are a few tips that can help you achieve (seemingly) effortless style.

✳ Wear a little *wool sweater* over your ball gown. There's nothing more kitsch than a stole or a bolero. Please, no stoles especially; even Hollywood stars have stopped wearing them on the red carpet. A sequined dress and a cashmere sweater—now that says Paris.

✳ Go to a discount store, but shop in the *men's* section.

✳ *mix* haute couture and street style: impeccably cut black trousers and a loose T-shirt in very thin cotton (youngsters can try something printed). When you aren't sure if you want to go luxe or casual, you've hit the spot: you're stylin'!

✳ Anything from a *surplus* store worn with old jewelry is good.

✳ *Layer* two scarves. This also works with two T-shirts, two blouses, two blazers, and even two belts. Layering gives the most basic pieces more importance.

THE UNIVERSAL GOLDEN RULE OF GOOD STYLE

If the bottom (pants, skirt) is loose, the top must be close-fitting. And if the bottom is slim-fit, the top must be loose.

✳ A maxi-*accessory* with a simple outfit. The Parisian has always admired Jackie Kennedy in her Onassis period: slim white pants, a black T-shirt, flip-flops—and oversized sunglasses. It's chic, it's efficient—copy it now!

✳ A *parka* over a little chiffon dress.

✳ *Pair* your worn-out old jeans with a silk shirt. This combination, just like the trousers and T-shirt, gives substance to the look. The rest has to be extremely simple. You have to make the luxury element—the silk blouse—look like an accident. If it's too obvious you wanted to make an impression, the effect is ruined, and you'll be accused of "trying to hard" to be stylish. Not cool at all. It's no secret: even though the Parisian buys stacks of fashion magazines to stay informed, she doesn't want anyone to know about it! She's capable of buying this guide and claiming it's to give as a gift.

✳ *Cinch* everything with a man's belt—something used and too long—and tie a knot in the dangling end.

What's the trick for mixing colors?

You can do it all! When things clash, it's called "color blocking." Although I'm a big fan of neutral, earthy colors (they're mellow), I really like navy blue (but not necessarily black). One thing is sure: when I wear a bright color (I love fuchsia), the rest is either plain or it's part of a head-to-toe pink look. But mixing neon pink and neon yellow is only for the very brave. See the difference?

✳ When you're tired of your clothes, dye them *navy blue*. It will give them a second life—unless of course they're already navy blue!

✳ Don't be afraid to wear your twelve-year-old son's *shirt* with a visible push-up bra. Or, the opposite: your lover's extra-large shirt. The idea is to try out sizes that you're not used to buying.

MIX IT UP

"Out with outfits!" should be your battle cry. Mixing things up and avoiding the obvious is the *Parisienne*'s favorite pastime. Two or three slightly absurd details can make for incredible style. But obviously mixing things up is not without risk. A fashion faux pas is forever lurking, but the Parisian always finds a way to turn her blunder to stylistic effect. She also knows that overdoing elegance is not a good idea. Always aim to upset convention. Here are my top ten ideas—from least to most risky—for mixing up your look, Paris-style.

10 mixes that match

① Jeans with rhinestone sandals ... not sneakers.

② A pencil skirt with ballet flats ... not heels.

③ A sequined sweater with a pair of men's trousers ... not a skirt.

④ A diamond necklace with a jean shirt during the day ... not a black dress at night.

⑤ Penny loafers with shorts ... and even socks ... not trousers without socks.

⑥ An evening dress with minimalist flip-flops ... not rhinestone sandals.

⑦ A pearl necklace with a rock T-shirt ... not a sleeveless dress.

⑧ A print chiffon dress with broken-in biker boots ... not brand-new ballet flats.

⑨ A tuxedo with sneakers ... not stilettos.

⑩ An evening dress with a straw handbag ... not a gold clutch.

FASHION BOTOX

A dress in a bad print will instantly age you.
Go for youthful looks—they're as effective
as those anti-wrinkle injections. And so much more fun!
How do you give your style a face lift?
Here are some solutions.

Change your style

Don't get stuck in a style after a certain age: that's what makes you look old. In fact, the biggest danger when you hit 40 is remaining stuck in your 30s. You've just reached the end of that wonderful decade when you feel comfortable with yourself, everything looks good on you, and life is full of possibilities and fascinating things in work, love, and family—you're both young *and* mature and you'd like for it to go on and on. In any case, you don't have time to think about it!

✶ At 40, to your great surprise, you start asking yourself this slightly surreal question: "Can I still wear that?" Instead of finding an answer, you're astonished to be asking. To be fair, it's still a little early, but better early than never! Don't cling to everything that looked great on you at 30. You've changed and times have changed, but so has fashion. You can claim to have a style, but boredom, lack of interest in new things, the absence of desire, habit, the fear of change or error—NO! You must be ready to make mistakes. Everyone makes a bad purchase now and then. It means you dream of being different and that's a good thing. Losing interest in getting dressed and putting on makeup is a form of depression. Learn to question your style as you get older. You're not changing, just evolving.

Golden rule
1

Never follow convention.

Never be boring.

Never let yourself go.

Golden rule
2

Always look for the right
accessory that will
transform your look.

EXAMPLE

Although I often wear
a navy blue, black, or
white shirt, I might
also suddenly slip on
a fuchsia pink blouse
and surprise everyone.
Now people stop trying
to figure out how old I am!

Follow this advice

① Cultivate curiosity.

This is a good way to stay young. Look for new brands, try new styles of trousers, climb into some wedges: be daring, even if it means committing a fashion faux pas!

② Sell your crocodile handbag on eBay.

③ Don't blindly follow trends.

✱ That's a rookie mistake. Learn to identify trends and adopt the most subtle: grey, wide trousers, peacoats. But forget about tartan, ripped jeans, and studded thigh boots.

④ Dare to surprise.

✱ In the evening, wear a leather jacket instead of a blazer and ballet flats rather than heels with a chiffon dress. Wear your brooch on your hip, or trade it in for a bold button.

⑤ Not everything you buy has to be interesting.

A nice scoop neck sweater is a must. You can wear it with jeans and a long necklace—it will look elegant without being boring.

⑥ Change your jewelry often ...

... even if you decide to wear a friendship bracelet!

⑦ Too chic is deadly after 45.

⑧ Never try the girly look.

Mini-skirt, funny printed T-shirts, etc.—you'll look like an old lady desperate to stay young.

9 *Penny loafers and ballet flats look good on everyone.*

A pair of sneakers (the *Parisienne* worships Converse) gives a woman over 50 a friendly, urban activist look.

10 *Get dressed while listening to*

"Dead Flowers" by the Rolling Stones.

11 *Clothes aren't the only things that can make you look old.*

Saying that Twitter is stupid, that you don't know how to use an MP3 player, and that you don't have an iPad will instantly age you. Even if you allow yourself to unplug, you have to stay tuned in.

12 *Don't be clichéd.*

13 *Always mix chic and cheap.*

FASHION FAUX PAS!

I've said it before: fashion blunders can
be redeeming. They can create a style no
one would have thought of. I think perfect
good taste is dull. Fashion changes every
season. You can abhor divided skirts
(culottes) one year and wear them in every
color the following year. The same goes
for jumpsuits, Norwegian sweaters, and
thigh boots. So it's not easy to identify
"fashion faux pas" under these conditions.
But there are a few looks that, no matter
what's in style, aren't flattering on anyone.
Here's a "best of" list of style bloopers,
according to the *Parisienne*.

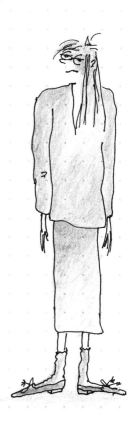

Lingerie

✱ Bras with transparent straps.
No one ever gets used to them. Wouldn't it be it sexier to let your bra show or just wear a strapless bra?

✱ Thongs with low-cut jeans.
One of fashion's mysteries.

✱ Visible garters,
unless you work at Crazy Horse!

✱ Pert and perky or well-endowed, **going bra-less is never ok.**

✱ Panty lines under a pencil skirt.
Thongs can be useful. For those of you who consider them instruments of torture, try seamless underwear (Uniqlo sells some).

✱ Nude tights.
Who's going to believe that velvet sheen is your skin? Just like those transparent bra straps, nude tights are hardly invisible. Stick with black.

Swimwear

✱ The too-sexy bikini in sequined lurex.
Nothing beats Ursula Andress's James-Bond-girl bikini bottom in *Dr. No*.

✱ A slashed swimsuit or one with complicated cutouts. You'll understand when you take it off after a day in the sun.

✱ A bikini bottom that doesn't cover your derrière.
The *Parisienne* gets a Brazilian wax, but she never wears the same bikini as a Carioca.

✱ A one-piece suit with your name on the chest. It's ok at your beachside bachelorette party or during a Tinder detox vacation (all while hoping to meet someone). But what other purpose could it possibly serve?

Accessories

✳ White fringed boots. The "cow-girl" theme has more refined options to choose from.

✳ A scrunchy in your hair. Too ditzy.

✳ White socks and sandals. If you're an American actress from New York starring in a *film d'auteur*, it could work. But it's practically forbidden in Paris

✳ Matching your tights to your shoes and bag is a big "don't".

✳ A backpack after middle school. Even if I do wear them from time to time—chic ones, in leather or canvas, or those famous Swedish ones (Fjällräven). But one thing is certain: purple and green athletic packs in bizarre shapes will never make it into my closet.

✳ Backwards baseball caps. In fact, is a baseball cap ever a good idea? Go for a sailor's cap or a straw hat instead.

✳ A bucket hat with a logo. You'll look like a sports fan. But if the hat is small, in a solid color, with a large brim, then it's fine.

✳ Plastic perforated clogs. I know thousands are sold every day, but I'll never like them.

YOU CAN CHANGE YOUR MIND!

Ten years ago, I really believed the fanny pack was only for tourists. Well, I was wrong: I wear one quite often now—even to cocktail parties. I have a rhinestone version for special occasions. But a gold or silver one is fine too. I guess it goes to show that, in fashion, anything is possible.

✱ **Sneakers with the logo in big letters on the outsole.** The *Parisienne* resists wearing logos, even though it's the latest trend. She doesn't pay to be a walking billboard for someone else.

✱ **Crêpe-soled shoes.** Get rid of these if you want to avoid looking like you're twenty years older and wearing a pair of slippers.

Jewelry

✱ **Rings on every finger.** As for the combination of bracelet + ring + watch + earrings + necklace—the answer is no, no, no, no, no!

✱ It wouldn't be going out on a limb **to banish the scarf ring.**

✱ **Piercings.** Looks too "no future."

✱ **Plastic jewelry.** Just bad taste in a world where plastic is no longer fantastic.

Fashion faux pas for the 50+ set

⟶ **Conventional clichés** (pearl necklace + earrings) No need to explain.

⟶ **Fur** Cruella is lurking. In addition to looking like you're flaunting your husband's wealth, fur makes you look ten years older!

⟶ **Mini-skirt and micro-shorts** Much like hanging on to your sippy-cup past pre-school.

⟶ **Certain neon pieces** I love neon colors. For example, a neon pink sweater around the waist can brighten up a white outfit. So obviously when I say "certain pieces," that means "no" to the neon Lycra dress that you found at a market near your place, but "yes" to a neon pink Indian shawl that you could wear to an al fresco dinner.

Clothes

✱ **A tight shirt** that forms holes between the buttons from being stretched over an ample chest. Choose something looser and don't button it all the way up if you want to avoid blow-outs.

✱ **The leather suit.** Even if leather is popular, even if Angelina Jolie wore one, even if you see it in all the magazines: you can try a jacket or trousers, but not a jacket and trousers. Too showbiz.

✱ **Fishnet T-shirts.** Except for Madonna in her *Desperately Seeking Susan* phase, no one ever really looks good in this.

✱ **Cropped T-shirts.** Revealing your belly button anywhere but the beach is never chic. It's a matter of proportion. And let me remind anyone who says otherwise: Gigi Hadid is not Parisian.

✱ **A leopard dress with a plunging neckline.** Too sexy is just too much.

✱ **Nightshirts printed with children's cartoon characters.** I've never see a man awestruck by a Hello Kitty nightgown.

✱ **See-through trousers.** What's the point of wearing trousers if you're going to reveal everything?

✱ **T-shirts with supposedly funny sayings** like "My boyfriend isn't in Paris right now" or "I'm looking for a rich husband." Do I really need to explain?

✱ **Mixing too many materials:** satin + velvet + chiffon + tweed = fabric overdose.

✱ **Leggings.** They're rarely becoming.

Top 5 Things to Avoid

(don't) *The counterfeit bag.*

There's nothing stylish about prancing around
with an imitation luxury bag, especially since you
have no idea under what conditions it was made.
A cotton tote bag or a simple leather bag without
a logo is much more authentic.

(don't) *Bermuda shorts with pockets.*

Have you ever seen a pair on the runway?
No, not if you think of the brands we like.
That surely means something.

(don't) *The Lycra bra.*

Either you're a *Flashdance* performer
or you don't wear one.

(don't) *The all-denim look.*

Unless you're in a Levi's ad, wearing denim
from head to toe will only remind people
of Britney Spears—and that's not very
Parisian at all.

(don't) *mixing stripes.*

Ok, you can combine a maximum of two in a look.
But copying fashion magazines that say anything
is possible, that you can combine three different
stripes in the same outfit, is just fashion suicide.

FASHION EMERGENCIES

A surprise dinner with friends? A wedding? A weekend in the country? The *Parisienne* realizes just hours before an event that she'll have to make a fashion effort. What can you do to boost your style in five minutes flat? There's a style solution for every situation.

A cocktail party

The setting

✱ **Every Parisian has been invited at least once to a cocktail party in an art gallery, or at a literary awards ceremony or store opening.**

Dress code

⟶ This is the moment to get out your tuxedo jacket (with black trousers, white jeans, or worn denim) and add a bold accessory (neon clutch, huge earrings, an enormous cuff bracelet). The goal: to blend into any arty setting. You could also get out your little black dress for the occasion. The best length? At the knees or just under the knees. Under-40s can try something shorter—that always looks pretty.

An evening with a potential boyfriend

The setting

✱ **Whether a Tinder date or your first evening out together: the goal is seduction.**

Dress code

⟶ The *Parisienne* is irritated by anything too obvious. Revealing too much on a first date with a plunging neck line and a miniskirt really isn't her style. In winter, she might even wear a turtleneck. A man's white button-up shirt and black trousers (or ⅞ cropped trousers for something more fun) and low-profile shoes will let your candidate concentrate on what you have to say. And lingerie? Ok, I'll admit it: a slight push-up bra can help—provided it isn't visible!

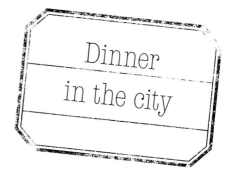

Dinner in the city

The setting

✱ **Some friends have invited you to dinner at a trendy restaurant. How do you look fashionable without trying too hard?**

Dress code

⟶ Stick to the basics and, above all, no flouncy dresses. Keep it simple if you don't know the restaurant's dress code (it might be very chic or super trendy, you never know with hip restaurants). What can make the difference? Shoes. Try something original (a color, high heels, gemstones). If you're really off-base, you can always hide them under the table!

From office to club

The setting

✗ **You have to go from back-to-back meetings at the office to dinner at a restaurant + night club without going home. The dancing queen look is not an option. (Have you ever tried going to work in a sequined top?)**

Dress code

⟶ Go for the tuxedo: it's chic at the office and sexy at the club. During the day, wear a blouse or T-shirt underneath. Before leaving the office, take off the blouse or T-shirt for a very Yves-Saint-Laurent look (your bra must be black, like the tuxedo). Keep your black heels on. (Some girls might dare to wear silver to the office; it'll give people something to talk about at the water cooler.) And add lots of necklaces (you can wear them during the day too). Leave your big tote in a desk drawer, just grabbing the little clutch you had stowed inside. You're a professional! Superman couldn't have done better.

A weekend in the country

The setting

✗ **Parisians are often invited to the country for the weekend. How do they avoid looking like country bumpkins?**

Dress code

⟶ Get rid of all external signs of fashion. Leave the "It" bag at home and grab a straw bag or a cotton tote—or even a satchel. Get out the Converse and stow the ballet flats; take off all your jewelry, except for a man's watch. And focus on the basics (tank top, khakis, T-shirt). The only stylish piece allowed is a striped sailor shirt—especially if that particular countryside is near the sea!

Christmas dinner

The setting

✱ **Christmas Eve is full of possibility. If you want to try something a little theatrical, it's now or never.**

Dress code

→ Christmas can be fraught with family drama, so go for something cheerful. Neon pink, for example. For a glam look, wear dark bottoms, like a long pleated skirt or velvet trousers. And pepper your outfit with rhinestones (bracelets or a brooch on your belt, just not on your sweater). Ballet flats are perfect—it's going to be a long night.

43

A black-tie
event

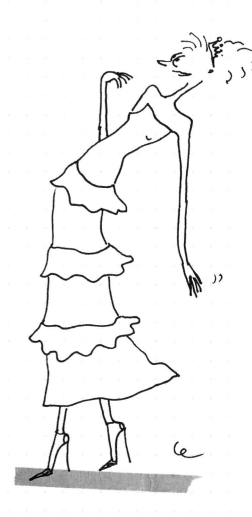

The setting

✴ **Everyone knows a girl obsessed with fairytales, who wants her guests in tuxedos and long dresses for her wedding.**

Dress code

⟶ Avoid the season's color if you won't have a hundred other occasions to wear it again. If you don't, you'll quickly find yourself blending in with the less imaginative guests (last summer coral was everywhere). The little black dress is always appropriate, so why not try a long black dress. To make it a little more fun, tie a colored ribbon around the waist. Parisians get theirs at Mokuba, 18, rue Montmartre, 1ᵉʳ,

tel: + 33 (0)1 40 13 81 41. If you're set on wearing a color, choose a dress in a hue you've always liked so you can wear it again. The key here is to keep it simple. Competing with the bride is never a good idea. High heels, on the other hand, are, but you can always go for flats—no one will hold it against you.

Dinner at home with friends

The setting

✳ The *Parisienne* is capable of fashion feats, but when she has guests over, she puts them at ease. She would never want to intimidate them by wearing stilettos and a little black dress. (*Parisiennes* rarely wear little black dresses with stilettos anyway.)

Dress code

⟶ The right combination? A subtly chic top and relaxed bottoms with flat shoes (normally you wear slippers at home). Add a stack of bracelets or a long necklace. And finish off your look with a lot of mascara—it's a way to dress up without being obvious.

A snack in the park

The setting

✳ It's rare, but sometimes the *Parisienne* goes out of her way to pick up her kids from school and take them to the park. If they're lucky to have an adventurous mother, this may even include a trip to the sandbox.

Dress code

⟶ Don't even think of taking a clutch: it proves you didn't know you had to give your child a snack after school. The outfit? Jeans, sweatshirt (a bright color, if possible; your child needs to be able to pick you out in the herd of parents) and sneakers. (Yes, I know sand is hard to deal with, but we're not getting out the flip-flops.)

Meeting the in-laws

The setting

✳ **Things are getting serious with your boyfriend, and he wants to introduce you to his parents. How can you look like the perfect future daughter-in-law without trying too hard (because they'll notice if you do)?**

Dress code

⟶ Trying to be too feminine is pointless; it can easily veer into too sexy. Go for trousers; printed silk is nice. In summer, wear a tank top and a little jacket (it says "this is serious") and in winter wear a button-up shirt. As for shoes, go flat (penny loafers are always a good choice) or for heels if you need confidence. But avoid six-inch heels; they're hardly appropriate for family reunions. You don't want to look like a call girl.

A visit to the Eiffel Tower

The setting

✳ **Tourist or not, when you visit the Eiffel Tower, make sure you don't find yourself climbing the grated staircases in stilettos.**

Dress code

⟶ If you're not from Paris, don't worry about dressing to measure up to the locals. You'll look most like them if you don't try too hard. Choose a relaxed outfit: jeans, a sweater, and a peacoat if it's cold. And make sure to wear sneakers: the lines for the elevators are endless, and anyway, taking the stairs is good for your health.

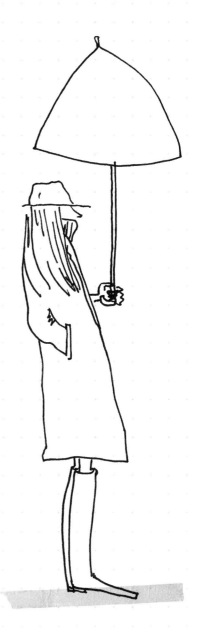

The setting

✳ **You get up and find out it's going to rain all day.**

Dress code

⟶ Ok, so you think today's the day to get out the trench. But contrary to what you may think, the trench does not protect you from the wind. So put on a sweater, a windbreaker, and then the trench. Better yet, wear a windbreaker with a hood. You won't have to worry about forgetting your umbrella everywhere you go. Who uses an umbrella anymore anyway, besides your five-year-old son, who only has one so he can open and close it for fun? Any responsible mother knows that only a windbreaker really provides protection from the rain.

PACK LIKE A PARISIAN

It's every *Parisienne*'s nightmare: figuring out how to stay stylish on vacation without packing her entire closet. Everyone thinks they're going to look like they just stepped out of a fashion magazine, but most of us just end up spending the summer in shorts and a shirt and something bought locally at a flea market. There's no point bringing your entire wardrobe; use this opportunity to enjoy the moment. But you can't leave completely empty-handed, so here's what to toss in your suitcase.

✱ No matter where I'm headed, I always bring *denim*. My go-to piece is a raw denim number by A.P.C.

✱ *White jeans* can be very useful, day or night—a bit like a little black dress. I like them slightly flared, like the ones I created for Ines de la Fressange Paris.

✱ Faded blue *work trousers*.

✱ *An Indian skirt* or jean shorts.

✱ *A loose shirt* in chambray or linen.

✱ **One or two long-sleeved T-shirts.** I like the ones 45RPM makes and the ones I buy in the United States at James Perse or Save Khaki. (I shop at men's stores.)

✱ **A kurta.**

✱ **A white cotton dress** works well at the beach and at the village dance.

✱ **A rather long belt** worn at the waist or the hips can save quite a few looks. I buy vintage versions at secondhand shops and military surplus stores (like Kiliwatch and Doursoux in Paris).

✱ Of course you can't forget **underwear (pure cotton)**. I'm addicted to Petit Bateau. Who says they're not sexy? The underwear's not supposed to be sexy—the person wearing it is. Wearing a black thong doesn't automatically make you irresistible.

✱ **Two swim suits.**

✱ I spend the summer in **sandals and espadrilles**. I love the ones by Rondini (rondini.fr) and Delphine & Victor (delphineetvictor.com), and I recently discovered Diegos (diegos.com), a French website where you can customize the color and ribbons on your espadrilles. After spending an hour testing red ribbons on navy blue espadrilles, white on red, and red on pink, I ended up ordering black espadrilles with . . . black ribbons.

✱ **One sarong.** I avoid bringing too many sarongs, hats, baskets, and small pieces of jewelry because they're more fun to buy on vacation.

Airport fashion

It's no joke: a *Parisienne* likes to look good at the airport.
Ok, she's not hounded by the paparazzi like the movie stars who
arrive in Los Angeles clutching their travel pillows, but even when
traveling, she has to maintain her stylish appearance under any
circumstance. Here's her checklist for flying in style.

✱ The Parisian likes to travel light. She prefers *two small nylon roller cases* to a single large(back-breaking) one. You have to resist packing your entire wardrobe. It's fine if you're an actress headed to Cannes and you need choices, but it becomes ridiculous when you're just going to lie around at the beach. Black is a safe bet in terms of color (yes, yes, leave nothing to chance), but everyone has a black suitcase, so to avoid looking like Inspector Gadget at baggage claim, choose something in khaki (by Périgot, a brand I love, a wheeled bag by Eastpack, or a soft suitcase by Bric's).

✱ *Socks,* to slip on after removing your shoes in flight.

✱ For long-haul flights, the Parisian wears *low-waisted jogging pants* in a loose material (cotton or terrycloth), never a skirt or a dress!

✱ *A large warm sweater is essential.* Wear layers underneath (from a tank top to long-sleeves) that you can remove once you arrive at your destination.

✱ *moisturizing cream,* lip balm, and eye drops—rehydration is key!

✱ *Sneakers* (Converse are best, in my opinion). Don't even think about traveling in heels or boots; if you take them off to sleep, you won't be able to put them back on, except maybe as earrings.

✱ *A very large bag,* like a tote, to hold books, magazines, and your computer.

What about a trip to the mountains?

I like skiing, but you won't find me in a ski suit looking like the mascot in a tire commercial. I ski in jeans, which considerably reduces the size of my winter suitcase.

BACK TO BASICS

A good look is built on solid basics!
Parisian style is (almost) easy to achieve.
A man's coat, a trench, a navy blue sweater,
a tank top, a little black dress, jeans,
a leather jacket . . . : these classics
are all you need in your closet.
The rest is a question of composition.
What effect are you after?
How do you tweak your basics?
What should you avoid?
Here's a how-to guide to creating a
"made in Paris" look with 11 essentials.

The little black dress

All about the little black dress

The little black dress isn't a garment, it's a concept. It's abstract, universal even. "Little black dress"? In reality, what does it mean? Édith Piaf pressing her hands to her stomach? Anna Magnani in tears in Italian neorealist films? Or Audrey Hepburn whistling for a taxi? Each and every one of us has our own mental image. Today, we all own several black dresses, just as we all own several pairs of jeans: they're all different versions of the same thing. The black dress is an open secret for women: we know it will save us in any situation.

The desired effect

Simplicity, simplicity, simplicity…
and a healthy dose of elegance.

Celeb style

Add big black sunglasses (1980s style by Persol) and black ballet flats. You can also add long black gloves in winter. Now you're ready for *Breakfast at Tiffany's à la* Holly Golightly.

The stand-out

Suddenly, you see it: a single black dress on a hanger. It's meant for you. There's a little black dress hiding in every store, waiting to become essential to one woman's wardrobe.

The leather jacket

The desired effect

Counteract geriatric styles and rescue any look from appearing overly conventional.

Celeb style

Brown leather jacket **+** white jeans **+** silk top **+** high heels.

Mix it up

✱ Brown leather is tasteful.

✱ Wear it over a chiffon dress to counteract the "garden party" look.

✱ In winter, wear it under a coat: it will give overly sophisticated looks a rock vibe. Your sweater can be longer than your jacket.

✱ With a pearl necklace—mixing is magic!

✱ The more broken-in it is, the more beautiful it is. When you buy it, put it under your mattress for a few nights before wearing it—or walk on it. You can also buy one in a vintage shop if you want to get your beauty sleep.

Fashion faux pas

⟶ Wearing it with biker boots— you're not Marlon Brando.

The stand-out

The best leather jacket is as close-fitting as possible, with high armholes and patch pockets. You won't necessarily find it where you'd expect: I found mine at Corinne Sarrut during the sales. The brand no longer exists, but the subtle biker look is still as relevant as ever.

The trench

The desired effect

To look like you've always had it,
like a second skin.

Celeb style

With jeans, tuxedo trousers, a little
black evening dress—can you think
of any time a trench is out of place?
It goes over and with everything!

Mix it up

✱ Roll up the sleeves and wrinkle
the collar so it doesn't look too stiff.

Fashion faux pas

⟶ Military style: too literal
for this coat, which was originally
designed for the trenches.

⟶ With a long skirt: watch
out for the "tower" effect.

⟶ With a twin-set, pearl
necklace, a pencil skirt, and a headband:
you'll run the serious risk of looking
like a bore—unless you're sixteen and
you're being ironic.

⟶ Anything in polyester.

The stand-out

**Burberry, of course! Many
versions appear similar from
a distance, but without the
iconic lining—it's still a great
look, though.**

The navy blue sweater

The desired effect

Crisp, but not too serious. You want a clean look, but something more refined than a simple black sweater. Admit it: sometimes a black sweater is just too obvious.

Celeb style

White jeans **+** navy blue V-neck sweater **+** high sandals **+** leather jacket.

Mix it up

✱ White jeans: a match made in heaven.

✱ Black trousers: Yves Saint Laurent always had great ideas for combining colors.

✱ Wear it with flat shoes for a cool, laidback look.

✱ In the evening, add heels and a cluster of bracelets—more "clink clink" than "bling bling."

What material?

Cashmere, obviously. Expensive? Not really! You can find cashmere everywhere at a decent price. (Parisians raid the collections at the Monoprix supermarket.) Don't forget that cashmere is far more resilient than other materials that break down after multiple washings.

Fashion faux pas

⟶ You can't really go wrong with a navy blue sweater—unless you pair it with yellow trousers— you'll look like a logo for a Swedish furniture company.

The stand-out

There are many fine navy blue sweaters out there. I get mine at Uniqlo (and not only because I work with this Japanese brand, which pays careful attention to product quality).

A navy blue man's coat

The desired effect

A masculine/feminine blend that's chic but not bling.

Celeb style

Every Parisian has this outfit in her closet: sweat shirt, jeans, and sneakers paired with this super classic coat.

Mix it up

✳ Pair it with running pants.

✳ With white trousers and a denim shirt, you're ready for anything.

✳ A sequined dress will give it a festive flair.

✳ The award for best basic look goes to: a man's coat with faded jeans and a T-shirt.

Fashion faux pas

Catastrophic with a skirt.

The stand-out

Obviously you should find yours in the small sizes of the men's department. From Zara to Ines de la Fressange Paris to Éric Bompard, the banker's coat is defined by its simplicity (no flashy buttons, please).

The perfect jeans

Celeb style

Worn-in jeans + tuxedo jacket + patent leather oxfords + printed scarf.

What color?

✳ Sky-blue, worn-in, faded, and raw: these four shades will get you through all four seasons.

✳ A black pair is essential.

✳ A white pair is cheerful—then it's up to you to add your favorite colors!

When to wear white jeans?

Who says white jeans are a summer item? I highly recommend wearing them in winter with a navy blue sweater and ballet flats. They also work well in the evening: paired with a silver sequined jacket, they're perfect for even the most elegant party.

The desired effect

We used to own just one pair of jeans. Now the fun lies in having several pairs: sky-blue, navy, white, black—one for every season and mood!

Which pair?

Fashionistas continue to argue whether baggy or boyfriend is best, but one thing is certain: straight leg is the most timeless.

The stand-out

The best pair of jeans is the one that looks good on you!

The tank top

The desired effect

A subtle supporting act. The tank is there to accompany your look.

Celeb style

White tank top + beige trousers + man's jacket + penny loafers.

Mix it up

✱ Wear it with shorts, jeans, or even a skirt (especially a printed skirt).

✱ Pair it with a beautiful necklace.

✱ Wear it with a tuxedo jacket or a blazer.

What color?

Keep it simple: white, black, grey, navy blue, or khaki. Avoid bright green, even if it's supposedly in style, and red, which is fine for keeping track of your kids at the beach but not much else.

The stand-out

Petit Bateau, obviously! A staple of French fashion heritage and a must-have for *Parisiennes*. Try it in children's size 16 for a stylish, close-fitting look.

Fashion faux pas

⟶ "Nude" tank tops—who wants to look naked?

⟶ Tank tops with slogans.

The pencil skirt

The desired effect

Sexy, without resorting to a mini-skirt.

Celeb style

With a T-shirt: counteract the classic look.

Mix it up

✳ Wear it with a leather jacket or a bomber, but never a blazer.

✳ Pair it with a man's shirt, tucked in, generously unbuttoned, sleeves rolled up.

✳ With a chunky sweater for instant cool.

Fashion faux pas

⟶ *Working Girl* style: silk blouse, blazer, and heels.

The stand-out

Christian Dior was one of the first designers to include pencil skirts in his collection, and the label still makes them. But today, you'll find them everywhere.

The jumpsuit

The desired effect

Obviously you want to look ladylike, not like a mechanic.

Celeb style

With nothing underneath and flat sandals.

Mix it up

✳ Wear a belt with a big shiny buckle or something studded to give it flair.

✳ Wear lots of necklaces.

Fashion faux pas

⟶ Even if you've seen many women do it, Parisians will never wear heels with a jumpsuit.

The stand-out

The originals, the ones you find in stores for professionals— they're inexpensive, but also not very becoming. My favorites? The jumpsuits you'll find at Atelier Beaurepaire (atelierbeaurepaire.com/en).

The white shirt

The desired effect

It gives any look instant style.

Celeb style

With jeans and silver sandals—basic, but not simple.

Mix it up

✱ Wear it under a leather jacket.

✱ Wear it with a pencil skirt.

✱ Under a tuxedo jacket, you can wear it out in "high society."

✱ Under a peacoat, it looks serious.

✱ It makes an impression with an all-white pant suit.

Fashion faux pas

⟶ Don't try to mix it with printed outfits. The white shirt shouldn't be considered a neutral; it has a right to its own personality.

The stand-out

A Parisian will tell you that few brands do it better than Charvet (28, place Vendôme, Paris 1er).

The blazer

Mix it up

✱ Belt it!

✱ Roll up the sleeves—the best way to an "easy chic" look. It's even better if the lining is a contrasting color.

✱ During the day, wear it with trousers of a different color (denim always works).

✱ In the evening, match the jacket and trousers—black with black has worked for centuries.

✱ Pair it with a carelessly open white blouse for a subtly seductive look. A lace top, silk or shimmering, is chic with a hint of sexy.

The desired effect

Masculine/feminine—certainly not masculine-masculine. Learn to give it a feminine touch.

Celeb style

Navy blue blazer **+** white chiffon blouse **+** white jeans. A clean, crisp style that looks good on everyone.

Fashion faux pas

⟶ Never wear a mini-skirt with a blazer. Too much femininity and you lose the balance.

⟶ There's nothing chic about a blazer that's too big. Drooping shoulder pads are forbidden!

The stand-out

The tuxedo jacket by Yves Saint Laurent. Wear only a bra underneath, like the maestro suggested. Obviously not everyone can afford the YSL one, but luckily, given its success, affordable versions are available everywhere. Phew!

SPOTLIGHT ON ACCESSORIES

The *Parisienne* likes a chic look built on basics,
so style depends on accessories. Whether
you're tall or short, thin or curvy, there's nothing
easier to shop for. If you want to invest
in accessories, you can go for more
affordable clothes—no one will notice.
It's the accessory that counts.

Parade of shoes

Women project many of their fantasies on shoes, a symbol of what they would like to be. This explains why some women buy shoes they'll never wear. We want shoes like we want bags: we already have a few, but we can't resist the siren call of novelty. We know that a simple pair of shoes can transform a whole look.

Consider this

It's ok to have just one pair of shoes, but make it a fine pair! And back-up sneakers will keep you moving in case of rain.

Concerning heels

Many women think they will look more beautiful if they wear heels, which is completely false. Just ask a man. No man will say: "I would love you so much more if you were six inches taller!" Not to mention that many women don't know how to walk in heels. There's nothing worse than a woman teetering around like a tightrope walker! You want to look sexy? Being sexy lies in gliding forward, not lurching along. I know girls who have ended up on crutches because they were so desperate to walk tall before mastering the rudiments of a skillful sway. Practice at home!

Penny loafers

Sandals

Oxfords

Ballet flats

Every Parisian's shoe collection includes . . .

Black heels

Riding boots

Velvet flats

Sneakers

Penny loafers

✳ These are essential, but require some skill to avoid falling into conventional clichés. So never wear them with a pleated skirt. You can wear them with medium-thick socks and cropped jeans. And don't forget to slip a coin—the penny—in the front to bring good luck. I have every brand, including the legendary Weejuns by G.H. Bass & Co.

Sandals

✳ How does anyone get through summer without sandals? I certainly can't! The iconic brand is Rondini, which you'll only find in Saint Tropez or online (rondini.fr). K. Jacques, also made in Saint Tropez, is another option, and you can find them online (kjacques.fr) and in Paris (16, rue Pavée, 4ᵉ, tel. + 33 (0)1 40 27 03 57). But a real *Parisienne* will tell you it's always better to go straight to the source.

Oxfords

✳ When you want a classic style without stuffiness or you want to go flat without being too low-profile, oxfords are the perfect compromise. They look great with jeans.

Ballet flats

✳ The E. Porselli version you find in Milan (or at A.P.C., apc.fr). When you're tall, like me, and you're tired of hearing "Are you sure you need heels?" every time you wear them, you start wearing ballet flats 24/7. Luckily there's a perfect pair for every occasion!

Black heels

✳ You can go through your whole life with a single pair of black heels— so it's worth investing! Of course, some years call for rounded toes, while others for something more pointed. But if you choose an ultra-classic model (neither too round nor too pointed), you can go miles without having to trade them in.

Riding boots

✳ Worn with a skirt, a dress, or even shorts and tights for the under-35s, riding boots are the winter equivalent of ballet flats. Black or brown, they really have to look like horse riding boots to be stylish. In fact, I know a few Parisians who are really in the saddle when it comes to fashion; they buy them in specialized equestrian stores.

Velvet flats

✳ Mine don't really look like the suede kind worn by gondoliers in Venice; they're more like thin-soled velvet loafers. But most importantly, they're decorated with rhinestones or embroidery. Who says you have to wear heels to have fun?

Sneakers

✳ Today, even Parisians who don't rap wear sneakers with their dresses on Mondays. Any brand will do, though I'm partial to my Converse, which remain the "official sneaker" of *Parisiennes* aged 7 to 77.

It's in the bag!

Consider this

You're better off with a simple wicker purse than a fake luxury handbag. Counterfeits are anti-fashion!

It's nearly impossible to commit a fashion faux pas when it comes to choosing a bag. Anything goes, from animal prints to neon pink. Even sequined-studded versions are allowed out during the day.

*

You can match your bag to your shoes, but only if you're under 30. After that, it makes you look 10 years older!

The handbag is one of the keys to Parisian style. It can make life easier (with pockets for a cell phone, lipstick, a snap hook for keys, an integrated pocket lamp) or make it a living hell (a huge bucket purse where everything gets lost and even a cat couldn't find its kittens). So it's important to choose the right one. The Parisian chooses her bag because she loves it, not because it's in this season. She's not interested in the "It" bag of the moment: she's after something legendary.

The ladies' handbag

5
must-have models

The straw bag

The satchel

The big tote

The jeweled clutch

The ladies' handbag

✳ The *Parisienne* likes to say that hers belonged to her grandmother. But everyone knows she got it at Hermès.

The straw bag

✳ Your best friend in summer, like Jane Birkin in Saint Tropez. *Parisiennes* also use it in the city to mix up chic looks.

The satchel

✳ Gives a casual touch and the impression that you are "anti-It-bag." A satchel is often a friend for life!

The big tote

✳ A faithful friend for daily use. You can slip a clutch into it, which is clever if you want to go out after work and you can't stop off at home first. Take out your clutch and leave your tote at the office—no one's the wiser.

The jeweled clutch

✳ Having a sparkly bag in your closet is as essential as having sweet-and-salty popcorn in your kitchen cupboard. Sequins, rhinestones, spangles— any one of these glittering materials can completely transform a look.

Diamonds are a girl's best friend

Sparkling around the clock: who still thinks you should only wear diamonds in the evening? I have a diamond necklace that belonged to my grandmother. I wear it during the day with a T-shirt. And when people ask me where it's from, I say it's costume jewelry! Yes, I do wear fakes sometimes, but now no one cares!

Consider this

Don't combine your engagement ring, your tenth-anniversary ring, and the charm bracelet celebrating the births of your four children: your most beautiful piece of jewelry is your wedding ring.

Choose one in tourmaline by Marie-Hélène de Taillac or in labradorite by Adelline for something luxurious but not over-the-top.

There's no such thing as too much!

The Parisian shuns accumulation, but that doesn't mean she's a minimalist. She likes to stack bracelets and necklaces, but not both at the same time (unless it's summer and she's not wearing much else)! It's important to choose the same material if you're going to stack: all silver or all gold. Choose necklaces in different lengths to dress up a neckline.

The cuff bracelet

5 pieces that make an impression

The charm bracelet

A man's watch

Vintage earrings

Colorful gemstone rings

The cuff bracelet

✴ This always makes a statement on an outfit. A cluster of bangles is also a good investment.

The charm bracelet

✴ Especially when it's exotic in origin and you can tell your friends: "I'd love to give you the address, but a friend brought it back from India."

A man's watch

✴ Adds surprise to any outfit.

Vintage earrings

✴ They'll never go out of style, seeing as they're already 100 years old.

The gemstone ring

✴ A gold ring topped with a precious or semi-precious stone is timeless.

Forbidden

A large necklace + big earrings: it screams Christmas tree!

KILLER OUTFITS

"I don't have anything to wear!"
How many times have you said this?
Even fashion professionals sometimes
feel like there's nothing in their closet,
that they always wear the same thing.
But learn to mix things up.
These five combinations will
last you a life time!

The denim combo

The key piece

With jeans, wear:

→ **1. A peacoat.** The double-breasted buttons add personality.

→ **2. Flat sandals** to round out this straightforward style.

→ **3. A white T-shirt,** an essential piece that guarantees simplicity.

→ **4. A clutch,** guaranteed to give this low-profile look some style.

→ **5 and 6. An old watch** and **a brown leather belt.**

The evening combo

The key piece

With a tuxedo jacket, wear:

→ **1. A white shirt** (or a man's white shirt).

→ **2. Tuxedo trousers** (but jeans work too).

→ **3, 4, 5. Rhinestone jewelry** if it's a special occasion or **a long necklace** in precious stones, with an unbuttoned shirt, and **a jeweled evening bag.**

→ **6. Laceless sneakers** (not heels, far too predictable).

The "I'm trying a trend" combo

The key piece

With white jeans, wear:

→ **1. An animal-print coat** or outerwear in another trend (it could be plaid or a bright color).

→ **2. Black heels.** (Sneakers will give this outfit a daytime look.)

→ **3. A black turtleneck,** your best friend in winter.

→ **4. A satchel** that counteracts too much chic.

→ **5 and 6. A stack of bangles** and **a black belt.**

The workday combo

The key piece

With a black sweater, wear:

⟶ **1. Black velvet trousers** (a softer alternative to jeans).
⟶ **2. School-girl penny loafers** look professional.
⟶ **3. A tote bag** with room for a stack of files.
⟶ **4. A man's coat.** Regardless of the color, it has to be structured.

The "total mix" combo

The key piece

With a straw basket, wear:

→ **1. A leather jacket** (or a jean jacket). Rock or folk, it sets the tone.

→ **2. A light, flower-print dress.** Longer will look chic (although you have to be careful with the leather jacket).

→ **3 and 4. A long charm necklace**—always useful—and **a cuff bracelet.**

→ **5. Flat, shiny sandals** to counteract too much rock or folk with a little glamour.

The essentials

The perfect wardrobe doesn't exist, because we're always missing something. I've learned to reduce my closet—not only is accumulation no longer fashionable, but paring down also brings clarity. Here's all you need.

Denim

☐ Black jeans
☐ Raw denim jeans
☐ Faded jeans
☐ White jeans

Trousers

☐ High-waisted trousers
☐ Black velvet trousers
☐ Printed silk pants
☐ ⅞ cropped pants
☐ Navy blue sailor pants

Shorts

☐ Denim shorts
(for summer only)

Skirts

☐ Pencil skirt
☐ Long flowing skirt

Dresses

☐ Shirt-dress
☐ Little black dress

Sweaters

☐ Black or navy blue turtleneck
☐ Black, navy blue, or beige crewneck
☐ Black, navy blue, or beige V-neck
☐ Pink fuchsia sweater
☐ Oversized sweater

Sweatshirt

☐ Grey sweatshirt

Tops

☐ White blouse
☐ Plaid shirt
☐ Striped shirt
☐ White button-up shirt
☐ Sky-blue (or denim) button-up shirt

Jeweled evening bags

T-shirts and tank tops

- ☐ White or black T-shirt
- ☐ Tank top
- ☐ Camisole
- ☐ Striped sailor shirt
- ☐ Indian tunic

Jackets, blazers, and coats

- ☐ Leather jacket
- ☐ Jean jacket
- ☐ Black or navy blue blazer
- ☐ Tuxedo jacket
- ☐ Peacoat
- ☐ Beige trench coat
- ☐ Navy blue man's coat

Bags

- ☐ Satchel
- ☐ Straw bag
- ☐ Small ladies' handbag
- ☐ Tote
- ☐ Jeweled bag or clutch

Jewelry

- ☐ Cuff bracelet
- ☐ Necklaces for layering
- ☐ Gold bangles
- ☐ Rhinestone jewelry

Belts

- ☐ Black belt
- ☐ Brown belt

Shoes

- ☐ American penny loafers
- ☐ Velvet jeweled flats
- ☐ Oxfords
- ☐ Ballet flats
- ☐ Black heels
- ☐ Flat sandals
- ☐ Sneakers
- ☐ Riding boots
- ☐ Boots

Scarves

- ☐ Cashmere scarf
- ☐ Printed scarf

Hats

- ☐ Sailor's cap
- ☐ Straw hat

HOW TO SHOP

Yes, I admit it: I once bought a long dress that was a little too frilly. I wore it once. Then it made some fashionista happy at the thrift store. Who hasn't been tempted by a trend? To avoid making purchases that don't reflect your style, learn to prepare your shopping excursions and how to make the right decision, fast. Here are some strategies to avoid becoming a fashion victim as soon as you walk into a shop.

Should you listen to the staff?

✱ Although some might like to see you leave with the entire store inventory, others realize that the better their advice, the more likely you are to return. So, often, listening to them is useful. But there are five phrases that should make you flee.

● *"It's very in this season!"* The *Parisienne* hates buying what everyone else is wearing. She's aware of what looks good on her and doesn't give a hoot about trends.

● *"I bought it too, and I wear it all the time"* (a trick often used by car salesmen).

● *"It's meant to be snug."* They say that when the next size is out of stock.

● *"These shoes will break in."* Careful: you might have to wear them with ski socks for three months at home before wearing them to a cocktail party.

Too many trends is overkill

✱ The *Parisienne* has always given the impression that trends do not interest her. "Really, leopard is in? I've been wearing it for ten years. I didn't wait for the fashion hounds to show my spots." Actually, she follows trends closely; her skill lies in integrating them into her look without anyone noticing. To make it work, the trend has to blend with your style. Use common sense: if you have a classic style, don't shake it up with that silver skirt you saw in all the fashion mags. But you can adopt the ascot blouse that everyone's raving about. We all have our limits in fashion; know what they are to avoid a look that boils down to nothing more than fashion diktats.

Don't overload your closet
(in Paris, they're miniscule)

✱ On the one hand, you have quality basics and on the other, favorite pieces that infuse your wardrobe with fun (a belt, a bag, whimsical jewelry). Even on a modest budget, there are a thousand ways to create a nice look. You don't really need much. Better to have only a few sweaters, jackets, and coats, but of good quality. Don't aim for quantity—learn to eliminate. The "I'm saving this for when I paint the house" excuse doesn't work either. Learn to give things away. One thing is for sure: your days will begin better if your closet is spartan but well-organized.

3 questions to ask yourself before opening your wallet

Could I wear this tonight?
YES ⟶ Buy it.
NO ⟶ Put it back.

Would that friend whose style I admire wear this?
YES ⟶ Buy it (and give it to her if you don't wear it).
NO ⟶ Put it back.

Do I already have this pink sweater? (If it's a black or navy sweater, the question doesn't apply; you can never have enough of those.)
YES ⟶ Put it back.
NO ⟶ Buy it. (It might seem strange, but you always need a pink sweater.)

STYLISH ADDRESSES

Contrary to what you might think, the *Parisienne* doesn't spend her time on avenue Montaigne! Yes, Dior, Chanel, Louis Vuitton, Saint Laurent, Hermès, Céline, and other masters of French savoir-faire are part of her fashion heritage, but she also likes shopping away from the luxury thoroughfares. Nice little boutiques, of-the-moment brands, and legendary spots: here are my favorite addresses.

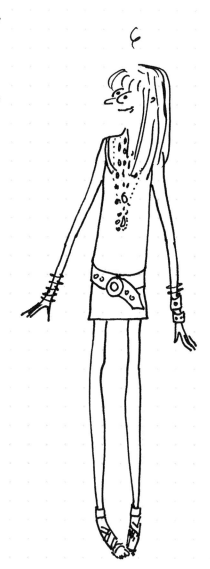

Clothing

Casey Casey

The style

✳ Minimalist, but not overly so. The materials are wonderful. This Paris-based brand produces fashion with personality. Everything seems timeless—refined simplicity made to last. Notably, everything is made in France.

THE TAKEAWAY

"Casey? Are you sure it's not Japanese? Issey Miyake could have started it."

The must-have

✳ The long cotton dresses, which are perfect for traveling, because they look nice even when they're wrinkled.

6, rue de Solférino, 7ᵉ
Tel. +33 (0)1 53 20 03 82
caseycasey.eu

Society Room

The style

✱ I like the fact that this store isn't obvious from the street. You have to know the brand's founders, Yvan Benbanaste and Fabrice Pinchart-Deny, to enter what looks like someone's home. But you're actually entering a custom tailor shop that makes perfectly cut suits and shirts. What's Yvan Benbanaste's style? A cross between a London and Neapolitan tailor. Just my style. In addition to custom work, Society Room has created a ready-to-wear collection for tomboys. Take note: all the furniture in the house—which changes regularly—is for sale.

The must-have

✱ A piece made just for you!

THE TAKEAWAY

"I'll take a suit and the table."

9, rue Pasquier, 8ᵉ
Tel. +33 (0)1 73 77 87 62
society-room.com/en

Ba&Sh

THE TAKEAWAY

"I wore this Ba&Sh dress to my sister's wedding this summer, but with boots and tights, it will look great in winter. Practical, economical, and sustainable!"

The style

✱ Who else can say they've been supplying young *Parisiennes* desperate for printed dresses for the last ten years? Sharon and Barbara, the two founders of Ba&Sh, have succeeded in staying in the game while staying in fashion. When you need a feminine outfit that will look good at any age (the creators made the smart move of designing every dress in two lengths), you know you'll find it at Ba&Sh.

The must-have

✱ Any dress that sets off the waist and makes your stomach look flat (their dresses work wonders).

81, avenue Victor Hugo, 16ᵉ
Tel. +33 (0)1 88 33 50 78
22, rue des Francs-Bourgeois, 3ᵉ
Tel. +33 (0)1 42 78 55 10
59 bis, rue Bonaparte, 6ᵉ
Tel. +33 (0)1 43 26 67 10
Locations worldwide
ba-sh.com/fr/en
International delivery available

Ines de la Fressange Paris

The style

✱ Read this guide and you'll know what's in my store. In addition to my clothing collection (I do try to offer more than blue blazers and jeans), you'll find all kinds of everyday and decorative objects that I like. You're as likely to find a toy for the kids as you are a soap dispenser by Peridot (much chicer than the manufacturer's packaging). I never go there when I need to buy a gift, because I'm afraid people will think I didn't pay for it (hardly chic). But that's a shame, because it's full of ideas, and I never find anything as nice elsewhere.

The must-have

✱ It's hard to choose. I'm tempted to say "everything." I'm often told the trousers are well-made.

THE TAKEAWAY

"Should I get a bracelet or a broom?"

24, rue de Grenelle, 6ᵉ
Tel. +33 (0)1 45 48 19 06
inesdelafressange.fr/en
International delivery available

The Place London

The style

✱ Although the *Parisienne* mainly buys her clothes in Paris, she is known to keep tabs on what's happening in London—for example, at this store, created by Simon Burstein, who worked in fashion. Son of the creators of the multilabel store Browns that was acquired by Farfetch, he was also director at Sonia Rykiel for more than twenty years. You'll find a collection of brands adored by English and French women alike (Sofie d'Hoore, Stouls, Laurence Dacade). The Place London also has a store in London (on Connaught Street) and this is its third location. Did someone say Brexit?

The must-have

✱ The flared velvet trousers by New Man. The symbol of a decade!

THE TAKEAWAY

"You don't need to go to London. You'll find all the brands you need right here!"

8, rue de l'Odéon, 6ᵉ
Tel. +33 (0) 1 40 51 01 51
London: 27 Connaught Street, W2 2AY
theplacelondon.co.uk
International delivery available

Bella Jones

The style

✱ This store is in a neighborhood where I wander often—rue Jacob—but I only recently discovered it. It's the first actual store for this brand created by Sylvie Sonsino. I like this kind of place, with everyday clothes that are easy to wear and yet timeless. It's the perfect place to shop for girls like me who are too old to dress like teenagers. It has a bohemian chic vibe—this is where you'll find the *Parisienne* style that people say is everywhere, except Paris!

The must-have

✱ The velvet jackets and trousers. The perfectly cut printed pants.

THE TAKEAWAY

"This store is located where the legendary Bar Vert used to be, a Saint-Germain haunt popular with Juliette Greco and Boris Vian."

14, rue Jacob, 6ᵉ
Tel. +33 (0)9 83 22 39 85
Locations worldwide
bellajones.eu
International delivery available

Atelier Beaurepaire

THE TAKEAWAY

"Accessorize your jumpsuit. I wear mine with a little red, white, and blue belt. That's handiwork too!"

The style

✱ Jumpsuits are always practical on the weekend: you never know when you'll need to lend a hand with a home improvement project. Even if you're not very handy, the right clothes will help you look the part! I found mine at this store near Canal Saint-Martin.

The must-have

✱ Obviously the unisex jumpsuit, called Ohlala.

28, rue Beaurepaire, 10ᵉ
Tel. +33 (0)1 42 08 17 03
atelierbeaurepaire.com/en
Limited international delivery

Sandra Serraf

The style

✈ I shouldn't be allowed into this multilabel store where I always try on everything and end up walking out with practically the whole store. I love the ethnic chic style that isn't over-the-top. The Indian-inspired prints are always beautiful. The selection here is charming: you'll find the collection Étoile by Isabel Marant, with Romanian-inspired blouses that can soften a blazer or a serious look, as well blouses by Laurence Bras and other brands that you won't find everywhere, like Xirena or V. de Vinster. The cherry on the cake? You'll also find jewelry by Pascale Monvoisin, one of my favorite designers (p. 109).

THE TAKEAWAY

"Sandra discovers designers that the fashion magazines will be fawning over two years from now!"

The must-have

✈ It's impossible to choose only one. I like the perfectly cut, soft, loose trousers with unique prints by Siyu. They pack easily and are perfect in the evening with an accessory or two.

18, rue Mabillon, 6ᵉ
Tel. +33 (0)1 43 25 21 24
sandraserraf.fr

Simone

The style

✱ This is one of my very favorite stores. It wasn't in the first edition of *Parisian Chic*, and this address alone was worth the reprint! I go for the original selection that you won't find anywhere else. Even the colors of the sweaters are unique. I particularly like the brand Laura Urbinati; her swimsuits are really beautiful. But everyone will find something here, especially those in search of colors that diverge from seasonal diktats.

THE TAKEAWAY

"There's no one named Simone here, but it's a good way to remember the name of this street where no one ever goes!"

The must-have

✱ Since things are always changing at Simone, it's hard to recommend a single piece. Just act fast when you see something you like.

1, rue Saint-Simon, 7ᵉ
Tel. +33 (0)1 42 22 81 40
simoneruesaintsimon.com

From Future

The style

✱ This new brand is shaking up cashmere. There's nothing revolutionary about the cut, which is my kind of modern (well, there are a few shorter sweaters that my daughter loves), but the colors are unusual: lapis lazuli blue, and neon orange, purple, and pink—just the hues we were waiting for in soft sweaters. Obviously more classic colors are also available. Although its main business is via its website, the store on rue de Rennes is very pleasant; the sweaters are all displayed and organized by thread count. The best part? These sweaters are not exorbitantly priced: 99€ (around $110 or £90) for six-thread-count. Unbeatable for this kind of quality!

The must-have

✱ My favorite is the crewneck raglan, which was already out of stock in yellow.

54, rue de Rennes, 6ᵉ
Tel. +33 (0)1 43 21 22 30
fromfuture.com

Centre Commercial

The style

✱ I'm always tempted to go here whenever I have a free minute. Men will find an array of hipster chic attire (including AMI by Alexandre Mattiussi, a must for the Parisian man). For women, I love the small, stylish brands like Masscob and Margaux Lonnberg, and bags by Isaac Reina.

The must-have

✱ Veja sneakers, which respect both humans and the planet. The brand was created in 2004 by one of the founders of Centre Commercial.

THE TAKEAWAY

"You'll also find Dr. Bronner soap, candles, books, and tableware. As the name suggests, it really has everything a shopping mall does!"

9, rue Madame, 6ᵉ
Tel. +33 (0)9 63 52 01 79
centrecommercial.cc/en
International delivery available

By Marie

The style

✱ Marie Gas has an eye for combining brands in ways that no one else would. Her multilabel store, with locations in Paris, Saint-Tropez, and Marseille, has a spark of personality that makes it essential for fashion fans around the world. She has a talent for discovering designers that will soon become famous. From Ancient Greek Sandals to Rue de Verneuil to Tooshie swimsuits, I want it all.

The must-have

✱ "Locket" jewelry by Marie Lichtenberg, inspired by Martinique but made in India.

THE TAKEAWAY

"She grew up surrounded by jewelry: her father is André Gas, founder of the eponymous jewelry brand."

8, avenue George V, 8ᵉ
Tel. +33 (0)1 53 23 88 00
bymarie.com
International delivery available

THE TAKEAWAY

"On her Instagram,
Bess posted that you
should never complain
and be happy every day.
For that reason alone,
I shop at her store!"

The style

✱ This is the very definition of ethnic-chic. Everything is high quality and well-cut. The fabrics are incredibly pleasant to wear. Shawls, jackets, coats, blankets, napkins—you're sure to find something you like. As a side note, since Gandhi's days, the khadi has been a symbol of independence for those "waking to freedom," as well as an impressive feat of hand weaving, which creates a thin, light fabric. Bess Nielson, the store's creator, is a Danish woman who exudes joy.

The must-have

✱ If you can't decide, get a scarf. You'll wear it forever.

82, boulevard Beaumarchais, 11ᵉ
Tel. +33 (0)1 43 57 10 25
khadiandco.com

Soeur

THE TAKEAWAY

"I'll have to hide this
bag I just bought.
My daughter's going
to steal it for sure."

The style

✱ Created by two sisters—Domitille
and Angélique Brion—this store was
originally aimed at young girls. But
given how their mothers raided the
racks of age-16 blouses and following
their incessant pleas to make sizes
for them, you can now find women's
clothing in sizes up to a US 10 at Soeur.

The must-have

✱ All the dresses are enchanting,
and the bags are impossible to resist!

88, rue Bonaparte, 6ᵉ
Tel. +33 (0)1 46 34 19 33
12, boulevard des Filles du Calvaire, 11ᵉ
Tel. +33 (0)1 58 30 90 96
soeur.fr/en
International delivery available

Isabel Marant

THE TAKEAWAY

"She released a men's line: I found lots of things for myself!"

The style

✱ Isabel built her success on ethnic-chic style. Embroidered tunics, loose pants, flowing dresses: it feels good to wear Marant. She found the style that suits the *Parisienne* best: quality, creative, logo-free, not too expensive, and as comfortable as a pair of jeans. Basically, every piece is a bestseller.

The must-have

✱ It would be ridiculous to suggest a must-have in this store; there are so many and they change every season.

1, rue Jacob, 6ᵉ
Tel. +33 (0)1 43 26 04 12
isabelmarant.com/us or /gb
Locations worldwide
International delivery available

Le Bon Marché

The style

✱ Rive Gauche style is concentrated in this fashionable department store. You'll find major luxury labels alongside up-and-coming brands sold here exclusively. The selection is very cutting-edge, and this is where you're likely to find that brand you spotted on Instagram. Beauty, decoration, books, menswear, and childrenswear— everything is painfully stylish and up-to-the-minute. It's the ideal destination for a day of shopping in the capital.

THE TAKEAWAY

"I'm going to apply to be a buyer for this store—I've been practicing for years."

The must-have

✱ You can't really go wrong here, because everything's been chosen by some of the best buyers in Paris.

24, rue de Sèvres, 7ᵉ
Tel. +33 (0)1 44 39 80 00
24s.com/en-us
International delivery available

A.P.C.

The style

✱ Basic but incredibly timeless. V-neck sweaters, cute dresses, bags, trousers—every *Parisienne* has at least one A.P.C. piece in her wardrobe.

The must-have

✱ The perfect straight-leg raw denim jeans. Whether turned up or worn as they are, they remain the A.P.C. VIP (Very Important Piece).

THE TAKEAWAY

"Even the new pieces look timeless."

112, rue Vieille-du-Temple, 3ᵉ
Tel. +33 (0)1 42 78 18 02
35, rue Madame, 6ᵉ. Tel. +33 (0)1 70 38 26 69
Locations worldwide, available at Harrods, Harvey Nichols, and Selfridges, London, and Bloomingdale's, Nordstrom, and Saks, New York
apc.fr
International delivery available

Eres

The style

★ It has to be the most difficult purchase to make: trying on a swimsuit is torture when you're in Paris, it's raining, and you're still carrying around that winter insulation. But it's always easier at Eres, because the suits are made in supportive fabrics that work wonders. The best thing about this place? The exceptional quality. I'm still wearing suits I bought here over ten years ago. Of course, durability comes at a price.

The must-have

★ There's a show-stopper every season, but the must-have is the suit that looks good on you.

THE TAKEAWAY

"Their Lycra is called 'soft skin.' That says everything."

2, rue Tronchet, 8ᵉ
Tel. +33 (0)1 47 42 28 82
40, avenue Montaigne, 8ᵉ
Tel. +33 (0)1 47 23 07 26
eresparis.com/en
International delivery available

accessories

Herbert Frère Soeur

THE TAKEAWAY

"I never should have shared this address. It seems like they're always out of belts now."

The style

✱ Simple bags with a bohemian-rock look that manages to be both original and classic. This brand was started by a brother and sister team who revamped their father's leather goods business in Brittany.

The must-have

✱ The Sab bag, which catapulted the brand to success, and the Line, also a very nice piece. Parisians wear the belts, but never say where they came from—they're afraid there won't be any left the next time they want one.

12, rue Jean-Jacques Rousseau, Ier
Tel. +33 (0)2 99 94 72 21
herbert-freresoeur.com

L'Uniform

Accessories

The style

✱ Whatever you want: Jeanne Signole makes basic canvas tote bags that are entirely customizable. Created in Carcassone, this stylish bag comes in several models. If you don't have the patience to wait for one to be made to your specifications, you can at least have your initials added to an existing model. Either way, my daughters love receiving these as gifts.

The must-have

✱ The small satchel is popular with all ages.

THE TAKEAWAY

"I spent the day testing different colored canvas online, but in the end, I went with black and white."

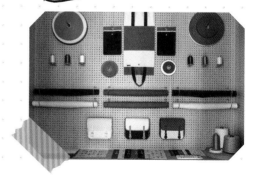

21, quai Malaquais, 6ᵉ
Tel. +33 (0)1 42 61 76 27
Locations in Tokyo and Taipei, available in Harrods, London, and The Webster Soho, New York. International delivery available
luniform.com/en-gb

Avril Gau

The style

✱ I admire the work of designer Avril Gau, whom I've known about for a very long time. Bags, shoes, boots, leather goods—everything is of the highest quality here. Her simple bags are as appealing as her wallets stamped with a rabbit, and the colors are always tasteful.

The must-have

✱ The bags are all very simple and the shoes have their own personality—it's impossible to choose.

THE TAKEAWAY

"Obviously I bought a pair of gold Mary Janes! I've wanted a pair since I was a little girl. No, I haven't worn them yet … No one has given me a sufficiently dazzling invitation, yet!"

17, rue des Quatre-Vents, 6ᵉ
Tel. +33 (0)1 43 29 49 04
avrilgau.com/eu
International delivery available

Jonathan Optic

The style

✳ I like how Jonathan, the owner, aims to make everyone look good in his glasses. This is no eyeglass superstore; staff look after customers, answering questions and giving advice. Buying a pair of glasses is difficult enough, so head straight to the pros.

The must-have

✳ Tom Ford, Moscot, Barton Perreira—you'll only find brands worth knowing about.

THE TAKEAWAY

"Don't tell anyone, but he also has a boutique with genuine retro frames (L'Antiquaire de l'Optique, 80, rue de Charonne, Paris 11ᵉ)."

17, rue des Rosiers, 4ᵉ
Tel. +33 (0)1 48 87 13 33
19, rue de Vignon, 8ᵉ
Tel. +33 (0)1 40 06 97 62
jonathanoptic.com

Roger Vivier

The style

✳ My home-sweet-home. This is where I work: for the brand created by the inventor of the stiletto. But it's also where you'll find the famous buckled ballet flats worn by Catherine Deneuve in *Belle de Jour*. They are magic: you can wear them just as easily with jeans or a dress. The famous buckle also appears in the collection of bags I design. If you need a shiny little clutch for the evening, you have your pick here.

The must-have

✳ Any accessory with a buckle will complete a look.

THE TAKEAWAY

"'Wearing the shoes of your dreams is to begin achieving them.' I didn't say it, Roger Vivier himself did!"

29, rue du Faubourg Saint-Honoré, 8ᵉ
Tel. +33 (0)1 53 43 00 85
Locations worldwide
rogervivier.com/us-en/home or/ww-en/home
International delivery available

Liwan

THE TAKEAWAY

"The friendly owner has amazing skin. She uses the Aleppo soap that she sells in her store—so I bought seven bars!"

The style

✱ This Lebanese boutique is so welcoming, you'll end up staying a while. Everything is exquisitely tasteful: large flowing tunics, jewelry, and decorative objects will give any white room instant personality.

The must-have

✱ The leather sandals in a range of colors and the belts.

8, rue Saint-Sulpice, 6ᵉ
Tel. +33 (0)1 43 26 07 40
Beirut: 56 Madrid Street, Mar Mikhayel
liwanlifestyle.com

Jérôme Dreyfuss

The style

✳ Jérôme's ultra-soft, super practical, and perfectly proportioned bags have become essential accessories. They're full of clever features, like a lanyard for keys and a pocket lamp for rummaging around in your bag in the dark. All the bags are named after men—falling in love is easy!

The must-have

✳ Jérôme's bags are named after boys, so you'll probably want one of each....

THE TAKEAWAY

"Did you know he did an internship at Ines de la Fressange a very long time ago?"

4, rue Jacob, 6ᵉ. Tel. +33 (0)1 56 81 85 30
1, rue Jacob, 6ᵉ. Tel. +33 (0)1 43 54 70 93
London: 20/22 Berkeley Square, W1J 6EQ
New York: 473/475 Broome Street, 10013
jerome-dreyfuss.com/us_en or /eu_en
International delivery available

Luj Paris

Jewelry

The style

✱ This brand has the full support of *Parisiennes*—the surfer necklace with turquoise pearls is a bestseller. This bohemian handmade jewelry also appears on the covers of fashion magazines. For the moment, the creator Julie Parnet doesn't have a boutique per se, but rather a showroom where you can book an appointment. If you don't have time to go shopping, you can order online.

The must-have

✱ I love layering the chain-link bracelets and necklaces.

THE TAKEAWAY

"I've known about Luj Paris for a long time, back when the designer didn't even have an Instagram account."

32, rue Notre-Dame-de-Lorette, 9ᵉ
By appointment only
Tel. +33 (0)1 83 89 56 23
lujparis.com
International delivery available

Pascale Monvoisin

The style

✱ More than simple jewelry, Pascale's creations are talismans and lucky charms; some people even say they'll change your life. But she doesn't put jewelry on a pedestal: she'll happily mix gold with seashells to form asymmetrical pendants.

The must-have

✱ The L'Amour necklace—but it's often out of stock and every *Parisienne* has one, so it's up to you to find your own must-have!

Simone necklace

THE TAKEAWAY

"Did you know that Pascale used to be an airline stewardess on long-haul flights? Her jewelry shows she's traveled the world!"

25, rue de l'Annonciation, 16ᵉ
Tel. +33 (0)9 63 57 89 91
pascalemonvoisin.com/en
International delivery available

Monic

The style

✳ There are thousands of pieces of jewelry of all shapes and sizes in this boutique. Monic is a magician who repairs my broken jewelry. She transforms it: she finds a way for me to use a pendant that I can't hang on anything and she can turn three gold baptismal medals into a minimalist bracelet. A friend of mine turned jewelry from her ex-husbands into ultrafine bangles—she was thrilled!

The must-have

✳ The piece she creates with your damaged jewelry.

THE TAKEAWAY

"Don't share this address with everyone.
I'd be annoyed to have to wait weeks for her to melt down my gold."

14, rue de l'Ancienne-Comédie, 6ᵉ
Tel. +33 (0)1 43 25 36 61
5, rue des Francs-Bourgeois, 4ᵉ
Tel. +33 (0)1 42 72 39 15
bijouxmonic.fr
International delivery available

White Bird

THE TAKEAWAY

"This ring? I don't know the brand; it was a gift. When I saw the box from White Bird, I knew it was bound to be beautiful."

Earrings by Charlotte Chesnais

The style

✱ A multilabel trove of charming jewelry. Minimalist or super-sophisticated, they're all tasteful and very creative. You'll find large rings by Pip Small, which I love. The boutique just opened a third location on the Left Bank. Hooray!

The must-have

✱ Charlotte Chesnais's jewelry is flawless.

62, rue des Saints-Pères, 7ᵉ
Tel. +33 (0)1 43 22 21 53
38, rue du Mont Thabor, 1ᵉʳ
Tel. +33 (0)1 58 62 25 86
7, boulevard des Filles-du-Calvaire, 3ᵉ
Tel. +33 (0)1 40 24 27 17
whitebirdjewellery.com/en
International delivery available

Stone

THE TAKEAWAY

"A word of advice: never show your daughter a piece from Stone— she'll steal it from you. It's happened in the best of families."

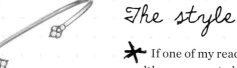

Sultane bangle bracelet

The style

✱ If one of my readers—a rather wealthy one—wanted to give me a delicate diamond bracelet, I would make her life easier by telling her to head to Stone. And if a fiancé wanted to offer a ring, he can be sure anything here won't be "too much." The creator, Marie Poniatowski, knows how to rock a diamond.

The must-have

✱ All the thin bracelets studded with tiny diamonds—and everything else.

60, rue des Saint-Pères, 7ᵉ
Tel. +33 (0)1 42 22 24 24
28, rue du Mont Thabor, 1ᵉʳ
Tel. +33 (0)1 40 26 72 29
Locations worldwide
stoneparis.com/en
International delivery available

JEM
(Jewellery Ethically Minded)

The style

✱ The way a piece of jewelry is made is part of its charm. JEM—for Jewellery Ethically Minded—was one of the first brands to focus on ethical production and earn the Fairmined label, which guarantees the origin of ethical gold, extracted from environmentally responsible mines. In addition to following an admirable philosophy, JEM makes highly desirable jewelry.

The must-have

✱ The Octogone ring, which works as an engagement ring.

THE TAKEAWAY

"Her fiancé gave her a JEM ring. That's a guy who wants to do the right thing!"

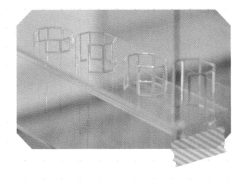

10, rue d'Alger, 1ᵉʳ
Tel. +33 (0)1 42 33 82 51
jem-paris.com/en
European delivery available

Emmanuelle Zysman

The style

✳ Quintessential charming jewelry. Emmanuelle says she finds inspiration in museums and art books. Her jewelry has a gypsy charm, and every piece tells a story. She can also customize and transform jewelry you already own.

The must-have

✳ The Honey Fullmoon engagement ring in yellow gold and diamond. But there are plenty of other little treasures in plated metal.

THE TAKEAWAY

"Everything here is made in Paris."

81, rue des Martyrs, 18ᵉ
Tel. +33 (0)1 42 52 01 00
33, rue de Grenelle, 7ᵉ
Tel. +33 (0)1 42 22 05 07
emmanuellezysman.fr/en
International delivery available

Marc Deloche

THE TAKEAWAY

"Marc Deloche is an architect by training and it shows: his pieces are well constructed."

Voltige bracelet

Nuage earrings

The style

✱ Min-i-mal-ist. Marc Deloche's jewelry is simple in the way that makes something instantly timeless and iconic. His pieces are so natural that when you wear them for the first time, it feels like you've always worn them.

The must-have

✱ His most well-known pieces are made of solid silver, but the gold Voltige bracelet is a good one to buy in multiples.

220–222, rue de Rivoli, 1er
Tel. +33 (0)1 40 41 99 64
marc-deloche.com/en
International delivery available

Adelline

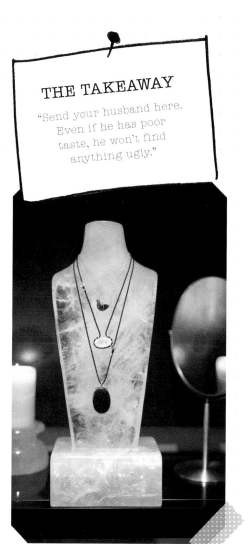

54, rue Jacob, 6ᵉ
Tel. +33 (0)1 47 03 07 18
adelline.com/en
International delivery available

The style

✱ Presented in a boutique showcase, Adelline's pieces are minimalist treasures that beg to be collected. Little *dormeuses*, long chains, and decorative heads on rings and bracelets: everything is tempting. With a hint of Indian influence (Adelline is inspired by the Gem Palace in Jaipur), every piece seems to tell a story.

The must-have

✱ That's a hard choice ... the gemstone rings are as irresistible as candy.

Marie-Hélène de Taillac

The style

✳ When you enter this store, you often hear: "I don't usually wear precious stones!" Starting with her first collection in 1996, Marie-Hélène de Taillac has been giving women the desire to wear "real jewelry" every day, pieces that don't look like they were taken out of the safe for a night at the opera. Simple and incredibly delicate, these jewels in precious or semi-precious stones have an Indian influence—Marie-Hélène creates her "ultra-luxurious bohemian" treasures in cheerful colors in Jaipur. Her renown has grown: three of her creations are in the permanent collection of the Musée des Arts Décoratifs in Paris. So chic!

The must-have

✳ Any MHT ring with a colored gemstone is highly prized.

THE TAKEAWAY

"Buying MHT jewelry is a bit like eating candy: once you start, it's hard to stop."

8, rue de Tournon, 6ᵉ
Tel. +33 (0)1 44 27 07 07
New York: 20 East 69th Street, 10021
Tokyo: 3-7-9 Kita Aoyama, Minato-Ku, 107-0061
mariehelenedetaillac.com/en
Delivery available in Europe, Japan, and the
USA, available on www.net-a-porter.com

ONLINE SHOPPING

A Parisian will always find a way to get in a quick bout of shopping, during her lunch break—but also just before bed. Clad in a nightshirt, mouse in hand, she can spend hours online clicking on clothes. Boutiques that stay open 24 hours a day, 7 days a week are a *Parisienne*'s dream come true!

World Wide Shopping

The *Parisienne* also likes to scout out what's going on abroad. New York, Los Angeles, London, and Milan: she doesn't need to travel to discover brands she won't find in Paris—as long as they stay in stock now that I mentioned them in this guide! Here are my favorite websites for e-shopping basics.

nomadicstateofmind.fr

✱ This French company offers environmentally friendly, fairtrade Mountain Momma rope sandals. Wear them with simple clothes. They're extremely comfortable but don't say I didn't warn you: your lover won't like them.

jamesperse.com

✱ You'll find the softest, most comfortable and well-cut shirts imaginable here. The colors are classic, but ideal: three shades of grey, navy blue, white, off-white, and black. The material is sewn on the bias, which makes them very supple. They're a little expensive, but worth it!

pantherella.eu

✱ My socks are cashmere; it's my daily guilty pleasure. I buy them in black or navy blue. This English brand has been around since 1937 and makes everything in its factory in Leicester.

lauraurbinati.com

✱ These swimsuits create a very pretty silhouette. You'll find them in Milan and on the brand's website.

thewebster.us

✱ It's been over ten years since the lovely Frenchwoman Laure Hériard-Dubreuil started her multilabel store in Miami. Since then, she's opened several other locations around the United States, most recently in New York. The selection is sassy, and she chooses pieces you won't find elsewhere.

WANTED

Do you, like me, spend hours searching online for something to wear at the beach without ever really knowing where to look? I finally found the site that's going to save me time, even though I know it's going to keep me busy: lyst.fr. It's a fashion-focused search engine that includes more than 1,000 boutiques. Now you can't say: "I looked online, but I couldn't find it!"

savekhaki.com

✱ Save Khaki United is a New York-based brand that excels in army-inspired clothes. The quality is out of this world, and everything is made in the United States.

mytheresa.com

✱ Everyone knows net-a-porter.com and matchesfashion.com based in London. Mytheresa.com, a Munich-based boutique, is just as stylish (it stocks over 200 luxury brands) and has the best exclusive offers. And I'm not just saying that because it carries Roger Vivier! Even better: delivery is super-fast.

Vive la France!

I like independent brands that can't be found just anywhere. Some aren't sold in many places, so grab your mouse and start filling your e-shopping cart.

delphineetvictor.com/en

✳ You can never have enough sandals in summer (they don't take up much room in your suitcase)! Delphine & Victor's are handmade in Greece and created with sustainable materials by craftspeople. Plus they're incredibly pretty (try the Apollines). Rest assured, I'm still a loyal fan of Rondini (rondini.fr), which I find fascinatingly minimalist. There's also K Jacques (kjacques.fr)—some of my friends are addicts.

charlottechesnais.fr/en

✳ Her jewelry is exactly the modern style that we need today. It's incredibly minimalist, but always manages to surprise. She works in plated metal as well as more precious materials. She doesn't have her own store yet, but you can buy her delightful creations online.

celinelefebure.com

✳ Bags by Céline Lefébure are simple and practical, but still pretty. Timeless.

rivedroite-paris.com/en

✳ Rive Droite was born from the observation that thirteen million tons of fabric are thrown away each year around the world and only two million tons are recycled. Whether it's recycled cotton, upcycled denim remnants, or stock fabric, the materials used for these bags are always fashionable.

jacquemus.com

✳ This young designer is incredibly talented. In fact, he doesn't need my support; his are some of the bestselling pieces in many stores. His website is a boon for those who can't access his work locally.

elietop.com

✳ I love Elie Top's original pieces, which look like esoteric talismans. He doesn't have an online store yet, but you can book an appointment with him in his Paris showrooms (217, rue Saint-Honoré, 1er).

IG styles

Yes, yes, I spend a bit of time on Instagram. Like you, if you're reading this guide, I look for style inspiration everywhere. Here are a few Instagram accounts that keep me up-to-date.

@street_style_corner

⟶ A street fashion account that proves right away that beige trousers with a white T-shirt and a black blazer is always a good idea.

@tommyton

⟶ A professional street photographer who captures hot looks outside fashion shows.

@styleandthebeach

⟶ If you really want to understand minimalism.

@stylesightworldwide

⟶ Photos of girls outside fashion shows—a front row seat onto the trends that are really on the street.

E-steals

The *Parisienne* loves to find a good deal.

theoutnet.com/en-us

✷ This is where girls go when they want a designer dress for a big event but they don't want to crack their nest egg. The website stocks over 350 designer brands with discounts of up to 75 percent. At this price, you won't find the season's latest dress, but didn't we say seasons are out anyway?

vestiairecollective.com

✷ Buying and selling second-hand clothes is the *Parisienne*'s new MO. At Vestiaire Collective, you'll find the brands you love at unbeatable prices.

collectorsquare.com/en

✷ Just like Vestiaire Collective, this website (which also has a showroom in Paris at 36, boulevard Raspail, 7ᵉ) gives luxury objects a second life. Specializing in jewelry, watches, and bags, this site is where you'll find the watch you've been lusting after at a significantly reduced price.

Part 2

PARISIENNE RIGHT DOWN TO THE FINGERTIPS

COMMON-SENSE BEAUTY

The *Parisienne* loves talking about beauty, but you won't find her spending hours in the bathroom. She isn't the type to accumulate a multitude of face masks and day creams; instead, she uses common sense—and follows these 12 beauty tips.

1 **During the day, the** *Parisienne* **might touch up her makeup with a powder compact she keeps in her purse.** But then again, she might also forget. At the end of the day, it's important to realize when your face is showing fatigue. It works like an alarm bell—a sign that it's time to go to bed.

2 **What's the most important beauty rule?** Remove your makeup! Even if you don't wear makeup, you should cleanse. And no makeup in bed. It's for-bed-den!

3 **Don't use soap on your face, or a lot of water.** A cleansing lotion or milk is better. Women who've been following this advice for years will assure you: they are far less likely to suffer from dry skin.

4 **There's nothing worse than over-primping before a night out.** That's so passé! It's better to look natural and fresh in the evening and save makeup for the morning—you'll be more radiant.

5 **The 20-something** *Parisienne* **examines her face in a magnifying mirror; the 50-something** *Parisienne*, **never.** Over a certain age, you're better off checking your overall complexion—always be sure your look still rocks.

6 **Don't use pink on your lips.** Transparent gloss is always best.

7 **Some shampoos are definitely better than others, but how you dry your hair and what you eat is way more important than any....** Oops, well, I guess I won't be signing any beauty product contracts, now!

(8) Don't go bankrupt on expensive beauty creams; the best beauty specialist is your dentist. A pretty smile and beautiful teeth can make up for anything.

(9) Avoid spa scrubs and peelings; they're too aggressive. A better choice is a walk with your fiancé … to Tiffany's. (Inside it's not too windy and a perfect environment for glowing skin.)

(10) Wear light makeup every day, even on the weekend. Just because you're with family, doesn't mean you can't look your best.

(11) Some *Parisiennes* can't imagine being seen without colored nail polish. But I think there's **nothing chicer than clear varnish.**

Consider this

Looking naturally beautiful has nothing to do with age; it's something you learn.

✗

I never go to beauty salons. I prefer meditating for ten minutes at home; it's less hassle. We never take enough time for ourselves—and that is really why we like going to the spa. Lying down at home for 30 minutes, doing nothing, is just as beneficial. Learn to slow down.

3 tips

⟶ Set your lipstick with a paper tissue.

⟶ Moisten your cotton ball before soaking it with eye-makeup remover.

⟶ Rinse your hair well.

(12) Never forget to moisturize your hands. They're just as important as your face is. I never used to use hand cream, but I fell in love with the Chanel hand cream bottle. I displayed it on my nightstand, and now I always remember to use it before going to bed. It can't do any harm, now, can it?

BEAUTY BOMBSHELLS

I often choose creams based on their packaging.
I like the objects I use every day to be beautiful.
I never buy cosmetics that come in unattractive
packaging. I love having pretty boxes and lovely
tubes in my bathroom. They're decorative and
keep things cheerful.

Throw everything else away—this is all you need!

Moisturizing Terracotta bronzing powder by Guerlain

→ There's nothing better for a sun-kissed complexion. What should you say to admirers? "No, I didn't go to the Bahamas, I went to Guerlain!"

Eight Hour Cream by Elizabeth Arden

→ This legendary skincare product always makes the rounds backstage at fashion shows.

Mascara by Guerlain

→ I look like a dead fish without mascara. These containers are miniature sculptures; I have one at the office and one at home. I only apply mascara to my upper lashes; wearing it on the lower lashes will make you look severe.

CAN'T DO WITHOUT

a toothbrush

It might seem obvious, but I'm surprised at how many people I see with yellow teeth. Toothpaste is a beauty product.

Body oil by Neutrogena

→ This absorbs quickly without leaving your skin greasy. And, of course, it makes your skin silky soft, which he'll no doubt notice!

Gloss by Chanel

→ Always looks fresher than lipstick.

Apricot nail cream by Dior

→ I apply this every evening before bed. It really hydrates my cuticles— almost better than a manicure.

Eyeshadow by Serge Lutens

→ The case is very pretty and the product blends magically.

Compact foundation by Chanel

→ Keep one in your purse. Most women need to even out their complexion, so a good foundation is essential.

Consider this

Everyone looks better with a little makeup!

My 10-minute beauty routine

✱ **For volume, apply mousse** or a supermarket volumizing mist to wet hair.

✱ **I never leave the house without applying day cream.** I buy mine at the drugstore and I change brands often. Go easy with it though: you shouldn't stick to your friends when you kiss them on the cheek.

✱ **Use liquid foundation** (in a pump dispenser—it's more convenient when you're in a hurry). I leave my compact foundation in my purse for touch-ups during the day.

✱ **Don't apply compact foundation with a sponge;** use your fingers as you would with a cream. It gives a more natural look.

✱ **No time for under-eye concealer!**

✱ **Apply mascara on your upper lashes only:** there's less risk of it running during the day.

✱ **If I have time, I smudge a little black crayon eyeliner** at the base of my lashes.

Consider this

PUT TOGETHER THREE MAKEUP BAGS: one for home, one for your purse, and one for the office. Even so, I sometimes forget to touch up my makeup during the day. I've learned that besides tissues, a compact Mason Pearson hair brush, and transparent gloss, I hardly need to take anything with me when I'm out.

REPLACE YOUR PRODUCTS REGULARLY: you don't have to keep that fuchsia lipstick that you never wear anymore, and your makeup case doesn't have to rival a professional's.

✱ **Apply bronzing powder with a large brush.**

✱ **Apply matte eyeshadow with a thin brush.** I use mostly shades of brown, but use whatever you like. One thing is certain: the more natural a color is, the more natural it'll look.

Fragrance favorites

✈ **Every ten years, I change perfumes.** I don't like contemporary scents, which I often find too aggressive; I prefer old-fashioned ones. I love Cuir de Russie by Chanel, from 1924,and Mitsouko by Guerlain, from 1919, which I like to wear every day. I don't like perfumes that smell like something specific, like chocolate, cotton candy, or citrus. But I do like blends that evoke amber, sandalwood, fresh roses, or carnations.

✈ **When you buy a perfume, always test it on your skin, not those little paper strips!** You can narrow down your choices using the strips, but then spray some on your wrist, leave the store, and spend a few hours with it, before you decide.

✈ **Perfumes are not trend pieces.** While some scents do become bestsellers designed to appeal to everyone, always make sure that your perfume is a good fit for your personality. In any case, the *Parisienne* avoids the fragrance of the moment— she prefers a hard-to-find essence that she'll cross the city of Paris for.

✈ **Never use too much; you'll give your friends a migraine.** The best pulse points are the neck and wrists, but so are the ankles and behind the knees. And always have an emergency bottle on hand in your car.

4 beauty secrets

⟶ **For glossy hair:** Three tablespoons of white vinegar diluted in a bowl of water, then applied to damp hair after shampooing, and ta-da—you'll shimmer in the spotlight!

⟶ **Drink carrot juice with ginger:** It tastes good, which makes you happy, which makes you beautiful.

⟶ **For a sparkling smile, use plaque disclosing tablets** (sold in drugstores).

⟶ **My vacation makeup routine:** During the day, a full-spectrum sunscreen is essential, combined with bronzing powder (Avène). In the evening, I use a color corrector (By Terry Brightening CC Serum) with mascara (Guerlain) and clear gloss (Chanel). I prefer a natural, glowing look, occasionally with a bit of kohl for an "I've been to Jaipur many times!" effect.

FOREVER YOUNG

My biggest role model in life is singer Julio Iglesias. Someone once asked him if he was afraid of getting old and he replied, "But I'm already old." The thought of wrinkles is more frightening at 20 than it is at 50.

I don't pay attention to my wrinkles; I just stand further away from the mirror. I'll consider Botox the day I see a good result. Up to now, I've only seen botched jobs. Plus, there are advantages to getting older. You learn to pack one suitcase instead of four. You appreciate the present moment. You listen to others. You put things in perspective. But that doesn't mean you have to let yourself go. Here are a few tips that might just stand in for an elixir of youth.

Consider this

To stay young,
stay light-hearted!

To stay beautiful for a lifetime:

- Be well-groomed.

- Smell good.

- Look after your teeth. Get your teeth cleaned regularly (every six months).

- Smile.

- Be indulgent.

- Be carefree and forget about your age.

- Be more easy-going.

- Be less self-centered.

- Be passionate about someone, a project, a house. It's an instant face-lift.

- Do things you enjoy. You'll feel at peace.

- Create an Instagram account to keep your finger on the pulse.

- Go easy on sugar, which damages the heart and blood vessels.

- Accept that there will be bad days, and make the most of the good ones!

And don't forget to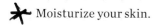:

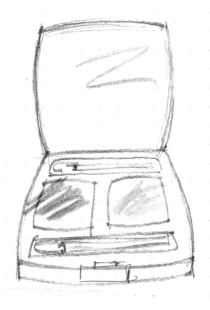

✳ Moisturize your skin.

✳ Use mascara, but skip the liquid eyeliner.

✳ Choose a foundation a shade lighter than your natural complexion. It will soften your face and reduce shadowy areas.

✳ Choose bright lipstick, or go for sheer gloss instead.

✳ Keep your nails short and don't skimp on manicures.

Consider this

You're better off spending an hour sleeping or making love than getting Botoxed at the dermatologist's.

Flawless makeup for over-50s

⟶ If you wear eye makeup, keep your skin light and natural.

⟶ You shouldn't glisten, but you don't want to look like you used the entire contents of your powder box either.

⟶ If you leave your eyes natural, use a bronzer on your face.

Things to be avoided at all costs if you don't want to look 10 years older

● *Too much high-coverage foundation, especially if it's too dark*—it screams "I have a membership at a tanning booth."

● *Going too heavy on shimmering eyeshadow*—it will only make your crow's feet more visible.

● *Leaving your eyebrows unkempt* and neglecting their curves.

● *Piling on the powder.*

● *Using brown blush under your cheekbones.*

● *Using lipliner.*

● *Finishing with a shimmery orangey-red lipstick* or a dull color like "nude."

And there you have it: the secret to looking much older than you really are!

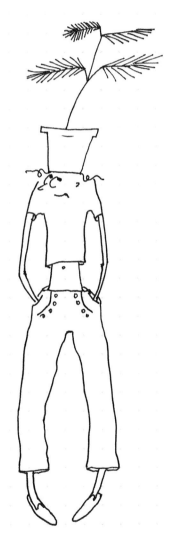

GOOD HAIR DAY

My one true obsession is my hair. It may seem like the *Parisienne* doesn't give a hoot about her hair, but that's all an illusion. She can spend hours picking out a shampoo or hair treatments. I've given this a lot of thought and here are my top suggestions.

How do you make your hair grow?

At the moment, I would love my hair to grow out quickly, because there are sections of different lengths and it's been tortured by too many hot irons, scorching blowouts, and too much hairspray. I'd love an easy-to-care-for bob. I've watched so many YouTube tutorials, I could write a thesis on the subject. Here are my golden rules:

First, prepare the groundwork: if you want a plant to grow, you need good soil. So use a hair scrub to get rid of dust, silicone, and everything else that suffocates the scalp. I recommend the Cleansing Purifying Scrub with Sea Salt by Christophe Robin. It's far better than kitchen salt, which some YouTubers suggest.

Wash your hair less often or use powdered jujube (the Paradise tree, but also known as Sidr), which you can find in health food stores. In a small bowl, mix the powder with oil to make a mask; apply it to your head and let sit for a half-hour.

Rinsing your hair with vinegar is a home remedy that works. After extensive testing, I've concluded that cider vinegar is best. It reduces limescale and makes your hair shiny. When I was a child, my nanny did this and it worked pretty well. I've seen tutorials telling you to use garlic, onion, or ground ginger, but what they don't tell you in the fine print is that some users may experience total celibacy for the duration.

✈ Your kitchen is full of beauty products: apparently honey is good for everything. Mix it with coconut oil and you've got yourself a recipe that will help your hair grow more than a half-inch per month.

✈ In the kitchen you'll also find mustard oil, which stimulates circulation and is good for growth. Miracle recipes for encouraging hair growth also include castor oil. It's a very thick, dense oil, but you can mix it with a lighter one. It also works for lashes, but the idea of having to apply it with a Q-tip just makes me reach for my mascara instead.

✈ Don't dry your hair with a hair dryer; use a micro-fiber towel instead. And don't brush your hair when it's wet.

✈ What's the best way to style your hair? Place rollers in your hair while it's still a little damp, apply a volumizing or lifting spray (Volumizing Mist with Rosewater by Christophe Robin is great), wrap in a scarf, check your Instagram, pay a few bills, order a couple of things online.... Then take out the rollers, run your fingers through your hair, and you're ready to go.

Consider this

Protect your hair with oil at the beach and at the pool, just as you would your skin.

If you want to keep it long

⟶ Don't cut it. To keep your ends from giving you away, moisturize them with a keratin-rich cream.

The best brush

⟶ Only use a boar's hair brush: the best hairstylists in the world agree. Don't forget to brush long hair every day—this draws sebum away from the scalp and down the fiber (yes, grease can be good).

The right cut

⟶ This one can be a real head-scratcher! The bob looks best on me right now (ok, I do need to let my hair grow a bit). You just have to try things out, and (normally) it will grow back. Like in fashion, the occasional change in style can feel like a change in your life.

BEAUTY FAUX PAS

As with fashion, we can all get it wrong
sometimes when it comes to beauty.
It's not about trends, but about creating
a harmonious look for your face. Although girls
on the runway may break out the fake blue
eyelashes, nude eyebrows, and metallic blush,
we live in the real world, without spotlights
or professional photographers, so don't be
too brazen. Even if you're a supermodel.
So, what should you avoid if you don't want
to end up a cosmetics casualty?

✳ Blush applied horizontally, like war paint. Make love, not war!

✳ Shimmery, shiny, and glittery makeup. Off the catwalk and off the magazine page, it's off-limits.

✳ Makeup that matches your clothes. It makes you look like someone who gave it too much thought but probably shouldn't have. You're better off matching your complexion, your eyes, or the color of your hair.

✳ Too much concealer + too much foundation = a muddy complexion.

✳ Applying foundation too quickly, without smoothing it all the way to your hairline. It looks like a mask and you'll be outed in no time.

✳ Over-plucked eyebrows. You'll be tempted to fill in the missing hair with a brow pencil and, quite frankly, that's not a good idea.

✳ Too much eyeliner—it'll make you look like a raccoon.

✳ A poorly executed "smokey eye"—a.k.a. the "panda look." If you haven't mastered the technique, skip it.

✳ Lipliner. This never looks good, especially if it's darker than your lipstick.

✳ Underarm hair. *Parisiennes* have a substantial budget for waxing, because *Parisiens*, as a general rule, like it smooth.

✳ Blue eyeshadow. If you want to look natural, this is not the way to go.

✳ Eye glitter. This makes even the youngest skin look old.!

✳ Mascara on your lower lashes. It makes you look severe and emphasizes under-eye circles.

✳ Too much gloss. A sticky-looking mouth is hardly becoming.

✳ Purple. It doesn't work as eyeshadow or mascara.

✳ Nail art. It looks ridiculous to me, even when it's subtle—a bit like a 50-year-old carrying a Hello Kitty purse.

TOP SPOTS

For product recommendations

My friend Dominique Lionnet knows all there is to know when it comes to perfume and beauty products. For many years, she ran a women's beauty magazine; she's a real connoisseur and I trust her advice. She makes regular recommendations on her Instagram account (dom_beautytalks), which is a treasure trove of beauty secrets and cosmetics to try.

Perfume

With the help of two noses, I recently created two perfumes for Ines de la Fressange Paris: Blanc Chic and Or Choc. Although I've worn the same scents for years, the process opened my eyes—or nose—to the many new fragrances that could very well lead me to betray my favorites.

Sous le Parasol

This thoroughly old-fashioned store has been around since 1936. The parent company is located in Burgundy, and it creates eau de cologne using an artisanal process. The grandfather founded this small business, then his son took over manufacturing, and today his granddaughter runs the shop. The bottles are as pure as the cologne. The Lotion des Tsars alone is worth the detour.

75, boulevard de Sébastopol, 2ᵉ
Tel. +33 (0)1 42 36 74 95
sousleparasol.fr

Atelier Cologne

✈ This shrine for eau de cologne addicts, created by Christophe Cervasel and Sylvie Ganter, works with the most prestigious perfume brands based in Grasse, France. Orange Sanguine, Grand Néroli, and Vanille Insensée have all won beauty awards. The candles also come in irresistible scents.

8, rue Saint-Florentin, 1er
Tel. +33 (0)1 42 60 00 31
Locations worldwide
ateliercologne.com
International delivery available

Le Labo

✱ I care a lot about the way containers look. Soap by Le Labo comes wrapped in artisanal paper and I like the scents: rose, sandalwood, bergamot, and neroli oil. The brand is also known for its perfume, which is custom-made in its stores.

6, rue de Bourbon-le-Château, 6ᵉ
Tel. +33 (0)1 46 34 37 65
Locations worldwide
lelabofragrances.com
International delivery available

Oriza
L. Legrand

✱ This one is a favorite. I can't help but wonder why I didn't discover this store sooner. I mean, the brand was created in 1720, after all. Declared an official supplier to the French court under the reign of Louis XV, it was also present in the courts of Italy, Russia, and Great Britain. How's that for exclusive? The products are of exceptional quality and the brand's only Parisian store is charming. Everything is ravishing and refined. The packaging is unique, the product names are poetic, and the original creations are extremely subtle. There's eau de parfum, eau de cologne, bath salts, home fragrances, candles, and even bath vinegar. Visiting this store is like stepping into a museum; it's full of old bottles, original illustrations, and inspirations. Plus, the sales staff is incredibly sweet and knows its products inside and out. It's been a long time since I've been so enthusiastic about a store!

18, rue Saint-Augustin, 2ᵉ
Tel. +33 (0)1 71 93 02 34
orizaparfums.com/en
International delivery available

BEAUTY MADE IN FRANCE

I have many friends who do things well. Take Lilou Fogli: she has many strings to her bow (she's notably an actor and screenwriter). With her mother and sister, she's also created a cosmetic and perfume brand that's "made in France" and dripping with sun (it's based in Marseille), called Château Berger (chateaubergercosmetiques.fr). It's still a relatively well-guarded secret, but its perfume alone is worth a look. It's become a must for many of my friends.

Guerlain

This one is legendary! Guerlain is the symbol of luxury French perfume. Here, you'll only find cult fragrances (Mitsouko, Shalimar, Habit Rouge, Vetiver) and perfume from the "La Parisienne" collection, a selection of rereleases of the brand's classic scents. Not to mention the famous Terracotta bronzing powder that gives desk-bound *Parisiennes* their sun-kissed complexions all year round.

68, avenue des Champs-Élysées, 8ᵉ
Tel. +33 (0)1 45 62 52 57
Locations worldwide
guerlain.com
International delivery available

Serge Lutens

✳ This is a magnificent place. Serge Lutens's perfumes all have incredible personality. I like wearing the spicy Amber Sultan in summer. This is a great place to shop for gifts: you can have someone's initials engraved on a beautiful bottle of perfume. Don't miss the adorable mini-format lipsticks that slip perfectly into a purse.

Jardin du Palais Royal,
142, galerie de Valois, 1ᵉʳ
Tel. +33 (0)1 49 27 09 09
Locations worldwide
sergelutens.com/us
International delivery available

Nose

✳ People call it a luxury apothecary. Right away, I could tell this was a wonderful place full of fine-smelling brands: you'll find names like Frédéric Malle, Francis Kurkdjian, Carthusia (perfume created in Capri in the fourteenth century), Comme des Garçons, Naomi Goodsir, and Penhaligon's. But the store's originality lies in its concept: with the help of a questionnaire (what perfume do you like or do you like to wear?), the staff will suggest a selection of current fragrances. How very practical!

20, rue Bachaumont, 2ᵉ
Tel. +33 (0)1 40 26 46 03
noseparis.com
International delivery available

Hair

I'm obsessed. I'm loyal to a particular hair stylist or colorist because I feel that a good hairstyle starts with a cut or color that suits my personality. If a colorist tries to convince me to go blond, I seriously doubt his intentions are good.

Salon Christophe Robin

✳ Christophe Robin is clearly one of the best colorists in Paris. His salon feels very welcoming and intimate. Rather than using the same colors for everyone, Christophe tries to find the ideal shade for each person. His objective is to highlight the complexion using hair color. I love his products: everything from the purifying shampoo with jujube bark extract to the temporary color gel, for a touch-up between appointments.

16, rue Bachaumont, 2ᵉ
Tel. +33 (0)1 40 20 02 83
christopherobin.com or .co.uk
International delivery available

Delphine Courteille

✳ This is my official hair stylist—a real pro who presides over photo studios and backstage at fashion shows, where she can let her creativity run wild. Her success continues to grow; in fact, she's moved to a bigger salon. She has what they call in the business "the touch": even women with the finest hair feel they've gained volume after Delphine's worked her magic. She's been awarded a National Merit medal. I think she's earned it.

PARIS EXCLUSIVE

28, rue du Mont-Thabor, 1ᵉʳ
Tel. +33 (0)1 47 03 35 35
delphinecourteille.com

David Lucas

✳ David has built his success on giving his clients exactly what they want—no mean feat for this talented hairdresser who could've let it all go to his head. He's put together a highly capable team, so no one is left high and dry when a last-minute appointment is needed. (If you want David, though, you have to reserve well in advance.) In his salon you'll find keratin-based products that he creates, as well as hair jewelry. The maestro also has a salon at the Hôtel de Crillon in Paris, one in Bordeaux, and a third in the sublime Ha(a)ïtza hotel in Pyla, where he's from. *Parisiennes* have made it their hangout to ensure a run-in with David at some point.

20, rue Danielle Casanova, 2ᵉ
Tel. +33 (0)1 47 03 92 04
davidlucas.paris
International delivery available

The Leonor Greyl Institute

✳ A spa for hair? My dream come true! There are anti-age, anti-hair loss, and reparative treatments for keeping your color bright. After analyzing your hair, an expert applies the appropriate elixir. Somewhere between a poultice and a massage, the treatments here will change your hair—for the better, of course!

15, rue Tronchet, 8ᵉ
Tel. +33 (0)1 42 65 32 26
leonorgreyl-usa.com or leonorgreyl.com/en/gb
European delivery available

Laboté

✳ Custom botanical treatments—now that's what I call true twenty-first-century cosmetics. Here, you fill out a questionnaire and pharmacists concoct a personalized treatment using ingredients made from medicinal plants. If you don't live in Paris, you can do it online. How great is that?

11, rue Madame, Paris 6ᵉ
Tel. +33 (0)1 45 48 97 48
labote.com
European delivery available

Cosmetics

Buly 1803

✳ This venerable brand, acquired and revived by artistic director Ramdane Touhami and his wife Victoire de Taillac, has quickly become a must. You get the impression that the boutique has always been around, despite its many years of slumber. Even the ceramic tile work has an old-fashioned, traditional feel. All the beauty products (creams, oils, perfumes, soaps, and more) and incense by Buly 1803 are lauded by those who use them. I love it here, but I go mostly for the Japanese makeup brushes. If you want to sound in-the-know, tell people that perfumer Jean-Vincent Buly inspired Honoré de Balzac's *La Comédie Humaine*.

6, rue Bonaparte, 6ᵉ
Tel. +33 (0)1 43 29 02 50
Locations worldwide
buly1803.com/en
International delivery available

THE PARISIAN HOME

INTERIOR STYLE

How do you give an apartment style? By sticking to a central theme. It could be based on a color scheme, a genre, a time period, or anything else, really. Compose your own moodboard by cutting out photos from magazines or scrolling through Pinterest to help you define your own personal look.

I like changing my interiors. The apartment where my girls were born was quite traditional and full of ornaments. Then I moved into a place that I decorated with a minimalist designer-chic look. For several years, I lived in a house with a garden that felt like a guesthouse. Today, my house has an artist's studio feel; it's located in Montparnasse, so I can imagine Modigliani or Foujita living here. I decided to use light colors and time-worn furniture. Updating furniture regularly gives your home a face-lift—there's nothing more depressing than watching your furniture grow old around you. Of course, there's no need for sweeping alterations or a major remodel. A few clever touches will do the trick.

Hide anything unsightly

For example,
put that drab grey printer
in the cupboard.

Drape fabric over sofas

→ There are two advantages
to doing this: it prevents sofas from
premature aging (I have two dogs!)
and it's an easy and inexpensive way
to change your decor (sofas don't
come cheap!).

Think white

→ Yes, I dared to paint a wall in
my office bright pink (it creates great
light and makes everyone look radiant!),
but I recommend white for small
apartments. As a general rule, if you're
hesitating between colors, go white.
To give a small apartment loft-like
proportions, color can work wonders:
choose a range of grey, beige, and khaki,
with black accents. That being said,
if you're in your own green, rose,
or blue period, you can always try an
accent wall. Worst case scenario, you'll
just paint over it a few months later.
In my new house, everything is white—
it simplifies everything!

Think inside the box

→ Boxes are a great solution for
small spaces. Parisians have many.
Put together a collection of zinc boxes
(muji.com) and stack them on shelves.
Piled high and labeled, they make it
easy to find things in a pinch: candles,
shoe polish, batteries, lightbulbs,
sewing supplies—whatever.

Keep lighting simple

→ Avoid elaborate lamps and go for simple spotlights. A single, original lamp can make a big statement.

Place scented candles in every room

→ A pleasant odor is just as important as pretty furniture. Light them as soon as you get home, even if it isn't dark yet!

Your interiors should reflect your personality

→ I'm a little schizophrenic: I love minimalist Zen style, but also colorful traditional designs. You can't approach home decoration like a film set: don't try to recreate a period style and don't worry about anachronisms. Mix things up, just as you would clothes. And combine cheap and chic. Why not put IKEA furniture alongside designer pieces or furniture you find at the flea market? I have no problem putting an IKEA sofa next to a designer lamp from the 1960s and a flea-market bookshelf that I've repainted. Remember: the total look is a no-no in home decor.

Display fruit

When your fruit basket is overflowing with oranges and apples, put a few in clear vases—it's practical and decorative.

Preserve your home's natural charm

→ Just as you'd respect a woman's personal style in fashion, respect your home's innate style when decorating. It's a crime to destroy period moldings in old Parisian apartments, but you can update by painting the ceiling trim pink, for example. In my last house, I created several rooms from a single space using greenhouse-style glass partitions.

Make your own artwork

→ You don't have to spend millions to hang art in your home. Frame your favorite children's drawings. I love all drawings by children under 10. They have a talent for free expression, something that fades as they grow. I give kids sheets of kraft paper and charcoal, and they create masterpieces I can frame. Magnetic plexiglass frames (Muji) will add distinction to any scrap of paper that's important to you, even a message scrawled on a paper napkin. Do the same with magazine photos that catch your eye: cut them out and frame them. There is no such thing as "lesser art."

Keep curtains simple

→ A single wrought-iron curtain rod is worth more than any faux-Louis XIV version. If you really want to keep things simple, don't hang curtains at all!

Make a "decor statement" with a chair or an armchair

→ Like a fashion accessory, it can set the tone in an otherwise minimalist decor. You can also make a statement with a lamp. Don't shy away from investing in a piece to define a decor—it's very effective.

Add a touch of humor

→ I like using ordinary objects in unexpected ways. For example, I look for dolls' china at flea markets to use in the kitchen. Tiny pots and pans are perfect for serving ice cream in—or sauces. A gravy boat is so predictable.

In the kitchen

Choose pastel-colored appliances

→ Many people think aluminum looks high-tech, but I prefer something softer: a light pink blender or a mint green refrigerator mellows the kitchen's mechanical side.

Harmonize containers

→ I display my spices, so I buy only one brand to avoid unsightly chaos, as they all come in the same bottle. I use Eric Bur, but I'm not their spokeswoman—you can choose any brand you like.

Be bold with dishware

→ I don't save my fancy tableware for special occasions. I like decorative dishes that I can use every day as well as for a birthday celebration. And don't be afraid of color. My dishes are red and white, and I display them in the china cabinet in my living room.

Store kitchen utensils in vases

→ Using ordinary objects in new ways is always fun. Be daring in decor as you would in fashion.

Let your table shine

→ Obviously silverware has its charm. But at the moment, I prefer knives and forks in matte gold. And you don't need to head to a pricey design boutique; you can get them at many high-street stores. I've even seen them at H&M.

Know when to leave the beaten path

→ I wanted my house to be totally white, so I wasn't about to install the same black stovetop as everyone else on my untreated wood countertop. With a little help from Google, I finally tracked down the seemingly impossible option in white.

Get rid of packaging

→ Pasta, rice, grains, even candy— I throw out all the cardboard and plastic packaging and put everything in jars. It looks far more organized, especially since my cupboards either have glass doors or no doors at all. I can find everything quickly and it's easy to see when supplies are running low.

Leave a copy of Dominique Loreau's book *L'Art de la Simplicité: How to Live More with Less* lying around. It's my decor bible and advocates applying Zen principles to life. Plus the Dalai Lama's *The Art of Happiness.*

In the bathroom

Simplify your soap

→ Instead of keeping those awful soap dispensers with logos plastered all over them, transfer liquid soap to plain bottles. Do the same with tissues: disguise them in boxes that match your decor. I do even better now—I buy shampoo and soap sold in minimalist containers, like ultra-simple Swedish products by Sachajuan or Volu shampoo by Davines.

Organize your perfume by brand

→ If, like me, you have several perfumes, organizing them by brand makes it easier to tell similar bottles apart.

Choose simple towels

→ At the store it's easy to fall for a towel in the same turquoise as an inviting lagoon. But be warned: it won't necessarily go with your bathroom tiles. (I highly discourage turquoise tiles.) Focus on one or two colors. All my bathroom towels are black and white. I order them from AMPM by La Redoute (ampm.fr). The colors never grow old, and if I need to replace a few when they wear out, I can always find more (I'm not sure "turquoise lagoon" will be on the shelves next year).

Flower power

Go for a Nordic spa vibe

→ Keep your shower mitt, or any other less-than-chic accessories, in a mini wooden pail.

Never use an actual toothbrush holder

→ It's hard to find an attractive toothbrush holder. Instead, I use ceramic cups that match my bathroom.

Let your plumbing shine

→ My bathroom is white from floor to ceiling, so matte black faucets add some depth. Plus, they never look dirty, so I don't have to worry about polishing them.

Yes, ugly bouquets do exist! But you can't go wrong if you:

🍃 Choose a flower with a long stem (a peony, for example) and display it alone in a beaker-style vase. Repeat as often as necessary. A white bouquet will always work well, too.

🍃 Plants are always welcome in the house, especially in black or zinc pots.

It's best to avoid:

🍃 Bouquets that combine flowers of different colors. You wouldn't combine more than three colors in fashion (and even that's pushing it), would you?

🍃 Forbidden flowers: chrysanthemums, which are a popular choice for tombstones in France.

🍃 Very long-stemmed flowers: no one ever has a suitable vase.

Or customize:

If the bouquet is really unattractive, divide it into several smaller bouquets.

14 decoration tips for a stylish interior

(1) Displaying a variety of ceramic items on a table is all the rage among *Parisiennes*, who swap the names of ceramicists as if they were insider fashion tips.

(2) Use tableware typically found in bars in new ways. I bought a few copper cups usually used for Moscow Mules (you can find them at 46, rue Sedaine, 11ᵉ or check online), but I just use them for display—they add a little sparkle to my living room.

(3) Whitewashed walls are always a good idea.

(4) Accept your obsessions: I like to collect things, but rather than hide them away, I display them—like the little wicker baskets lined up on my bookshelf.

(5) Leave some spaces empty or place a single element, like a sculpture. Especially if you tend to collect knickknacks.

(6) Leave a vintage stepladder next to your bookshelf as if to say "I spend my days looking for books. All I do is read."

(7) Display a painting on a mini-easel instead of a wall. It immediately makes the room feel more like an artist's studio. I'm a fan of Parisian artist Jean-Baptiste Sécheret's work.

(8) Group ornaments of the same color in a specific area to tie a room together.

(9) Choose large, inviting, comfortable sofas. It's easy to be tempted by the designer sofas you see in magazines, but when it comes to sprawling in one, they're not great.

(10) You wouldn't think so, but light switches can give a wall a makeover. At my house, they're mostly old-fashioned.

11) I polish my old wood furniture with plain wax, which you can find in any hardware store. It gives it a nice patina.

12) Invent new purposes for unused objects. That mug you never use? Fill it with soil and grow a little plant.

13) A string of lights brightens up any home, even when it's not Christmas.

14) If you have space, compose mini tabletop exhibits and mix works by different artists with Mother's Day gifts from your children—it's a great way to boost their confidence.

THE PERFECT CLOSET

A well-organized closet can change your whole outlook on life. It's not easy to stay organized in a small Parisian apartment, but you won't hear me tell anyone to throw everything out for lack of space; there's always a solution. Just follow Marie Kondo's lead. This Japanese woman, who invented the concept of organization consultant (my cleaner should have come up with this and asked for a raise), has already sold more than 2.5 million copies of her book *The Life-Changing Magic of Tidying Up* (Ten Speed Press). I follow a lot of her advice, although I'm not at the point where I talk to my socks to see if they "spark joy." Still, many of her ideas have led me to focus on the essentials. Here are my storage solutions.

Consider this

**Cleaning your house
is not a necessity,
it's an obligation!
It clears the mind and
improves your life.**

✳

**The city is cluttered
enough as it is,
so keep the mess at home
to a minimum.**

Photograph your shoes

✱ The best advice is to photograph each pair of shoes with a Polaroid camera, put the shoes in the box, then glue the photo to the front of the box. Stack the boxes like they do in shoe stores. For a less glamorous version, photograph your shoes with a digital camera, print the photos, and glue them to the front of a storage box (that way you can put more than one pair in the same box).

Invest in a single type of hanger

✱ Ikea carries black or white plastic ones that don't take up much space and can hold many things. Unification provides clarity.

Get rid of unnecessary clutter

✳ This is not always easy to do. I've been lucky to move many times, but everyone should make it a rule to avoid accumulating things. Learn to let go. It won't cost you anything, and it makes for a more chic environment than an apartment packed with useless objects collecting dust! Plus, I can assure you, it feels really good to get rid of things that aren't all that important after all. The hardest thing to do is to create an inviting little jumble to offset your minimalist decor. An old stuffed animal displayed in a plexiglass box in your living room should do the trick.

The golden rule of small spaces

✳ Small spaces are only livable if they're well organized. Find as much storage space as you can and use every last bit of empty space available (cupboards under gabled roofs, beds, stairs, whatever). The goal is to find a dual purpose for your storage solutions: for example, I managed to hide my dogs' food in a chest that doubles as a seat. And in my daughter's room, I created a kind of podium for her bed and turned the single large step into a big drawer.

Organize your jewelry and accessories

✳ I display my jewelry as if it were in a boutique, which makes me want to wear it all the more. I have a stand for my necklaces and display cases (by AMPM) for rings, earrings, and bracelets. I keep a little basket full of different ribbons next to my pendants, which allows me to create necklaces whenever I like. The best option for bags, if you have space, is to display them in a wardrobe, boutique-style; otherwise, I hang them on a towel rack (or a paper-towel rack) on the wall, which makes it easy to pick out a bag in the morning. And don't think I only own chic handbags; I also display my cotton tote bags, which can serve as handy file storage.

Learn to "edit" your wardrobe

✳ This term has a much more professional—and chicer—ring to it than "throw away." But it means exactly the same thing: anything in bad shape that you haven't worn in ages should go. If you don't have the immediate urge to wear a piece of clothing when you see it, get rid of it. If in doubt, think of a friend whose style you admire and ask yourself, "Would she wear this?" If the answer is "no," send it off to the Salvation Army for a second life.

Organize your clothes by category

✳ Put trousers with trousers, group T-shirts together, separate out sweaters, etc. Organize your clothes by season. If you want to take it to the next level, organize them by color! It makes for a more cheerful wardrobe.

Give everything a front-row seat

✳ This isn't always easy to do, but if you can't see it, you won't wear it. Organize your jewelry and accessories in display cases, like your own mini jewelry store—that's where you feel like trying things on, after all. Plus, choosing what to wear is easier when you can see what you have.

Marie Kondo's most important lesson: fold and store your clothes vertically

✱ This concept has had the biggest influence on my closet. I used to like the idea of stacks of sweaters that resembled a store display. But that's hardly practical when the stack is more than two T-shirts high. Marie Kondo encourages vertical folding and storage. Once you've sorted your clothes, she suggests first folding them in a specific way (lay them flat and fold each edge toward the center). Then organize them in drawers, and if you don't have enough drawers, put them in boxes. That way, you can see everything, and you don't end the week surrounded by a chaotic mess. I've been doing it this way for several years, and it has changed my life!

China inspired

Before Marie Kondo came along, I was an adherent of Feng Shui, the ancient Chinese art of finding harmony in one's home. I follow three principles:

→ Don't put your office in your bedroom; areas for work and rest should remain separate.

→ Quickly repair anything broken or damaged, otherwise energy stagnates.

→ Display oranges and lemons around the house, as it supposedly brings good luck.

GREEN IS THE NEW BLACK

It's never too late to wake up and smell the roses!
Ten years ago, *Parisiennes* weren't fully aware
of the extent of the harm being done to the planet.
Today, we all know urgent action is needed. Because
I work for fashion brands that aren't always fully aligned
with sustainable development principles, it's hard
for me to be an eco-ambassador—right now.
But I'm working on it, and I really try to raise awareness
among the brands I work with. Here are a few habits
for the ecologically conscious to adopt.

Vallée
Village

I practice slow fashion

✈ I've always said: buy less, buy better. So, I prefer to spend a little more on a quality piece of clothing than to pay less for something that will fall apart after three washes. What could be more fashionably "eco-friendly"?

→ Buy vintage and sell your unwanted clothes

Whenever I move or reorganize my closet, I always donate any garments I've fallen out of love with to charitable organizations. It just makes sense. But for those who want to top up their bank account, there are an increasing number of online secondhand stores. Vinted is an indispensable app: it's the perfect place to sell that dress you got for a wedding two years ago and haven't worn since, or to get rid of a sweatshirt with a flashy logo that you bought in a moment of folly. Of course, you can also buy clothes that others are selling on the app. If you want something a little more chic—luxurious, even—check out Vestiaire Collective. The concept is the same as Vinted, but the selection is more exclusive.

→ Rent evening or cocktail gowns

To wear Alaïa for just one evening—and for a fraction of the usual price—there are rental sites such as Rent the Runway (renttherunway.com) or, in France, Une Robe Un Soir (1robepour1soir.com/en_GB).

→ Get a good deal with last season's clothes

We all get it—the *Parisienne* does not follow trends. So it doesn't matter if her clothes are from previous seasons. You can score some amazing deals at outlet stores. Vallée Village—just outside of Paris at 3, cours de la Garonne, 77700 Serris (lavalleevillage.com/en) and easily accessible via shuttle bus or RER express train—is really worth the detour! Designer labels like Gucci, Valentino, Prada, Tod's, Céline, Jimmy Choo, but also Isabel Marant, Levi's, Fusalp, and Zadig & Voltaire are all available at knockdown prices. In between stores, you can take a gastronomic break at Ladurée, La Maison du Chocolat, Pierre Hermé, or Amorino. Not only will you find great bargains here, but you'll also help save certain garments from extinction.

I opt for fine food stores and local producers

*When I go grocery shopping, I try to go as much as possible to fine food stores or markets that stock small producers. When I can't make it out in Paris, I click on epicery.com which features a number of fine food stores, including some that deliver meals; check in your local area for similar sites. I also like La Laiterie de Paris (lalaiteriedeparis.blogspot.com), which collects milk from around the Île-de-France region to make cheese in Paris.

I check out "healthy" restaurants

*Ok, so even though I'll suggest trendy spots for dinner—where earth-friendly measures are sometimes little more than paid lip service—let me tell you that I'm spending more and more time in restaurants that serve simple, often vegetarian, cuisine. Here are my three favorites:

→ **Vida** (49, rue de l'Échiquier, 10e, tel. + 33 (0)1 48 00 08 28, restaurant-vida.com). Created by the Frenchiest of Colombian chefs, Juan Arbelaez, and launched with his girlfriend, journalist Laury Thilleman, this restaurant serves only the freshest, most seasonal produce, and the decor is oh-so-inviting.

→ **Simple** (86, rue du Cherche-Midi, 6e, tel. +33 (0)1 45 44 79 88). This is the perfect place for a healthy lunch after a morning of shopping in the 6e *arrondissement* (it's near the Bon Marché department store). As its name implies, the food here is "simple" but extremely healthy.

→ **Clover Green** (5, rue Perronet, 7e, tel. +33 (0)1 75 50 00 05, clover-paris.com). This ultra-healthy restaurant was opened by Elodie and Michelin-star chef Jean-François Piège, who has written books on healthy eating and knows the secret for how to make asparagus soup addictive.

FIVE THINGS I DO FOR THE PLANET

- I never leave the water running for no reason; I turn it off when I brush my teeth.
- I use a mug at the office instead of plastic cups.
- I clean everything with white vinegar.
- I dye my clothes when the color has faded.
- I put gifts in a pretty reusable cloth bag instead of wrapping them in paper.

I only drink homemade fruit and vegetable juices

✳ I made up my mind about this after watching a documentary on Netflix: fat, sick, and practically dying, a guy decides to drink only fruit and vegetable juice for sixty days. He waxes lyrical about the effects of the diet on his weight and skin problems. I'm not out to lose weight, but it seemed to me that this diet also had a purely positive effect on his mental health. So I ordered a juice extractor (an Omega to be exact, which you can find online), and I immediately realized this is not your ordinary food processor. This machine preserves all the nutrients in fruit and vegetables to make juice packed with vitamins, healthfulness, and energy.

How I get around

Driving a car in Paris today is tantamount to saying, "Why don't I waste an hour of my day?" Traffic is so dense that it's just plain crazy to consider driving. So I walk. I'm lucky to live in one of the most beautiful cities in the world and I use the pedometer app on my iPhone. Walking is great exercise, it's good for the imagination, and you can window-shop at the same time!

DINNER PARTY COUNTDOWN

Everyone thinks that I host sophisticated dinner
parties, where I invite the crème de la crème of Paris.
But that's not me at all. In fact, when I entertain
at home, it's to spend time with friends, not to spend
the night in the kitchen. So how do you organize
a dinner like a *Parisienne*? Here's how I do it.

2 hours before

⟶ I run home after a day at work. Usually, I haven't prepared anything ahead of time. I have just enough time to buy a chicken on the way. I have nothing to wear for the evening. Magazines are piled high in the living room and the "big kids'" mess is strewn everywhere.

1 ½ hours to go

⟶ I put the chicken in a crockpot with whatever I can find in the kitchen— peeled tomatoes, onions, lots of herbs and spices like curry, cilantro, and thyme—and I let the whole thing simmer on low. While the chicken is cooking, I tidy up. And I take a bath.

1 hour to go

⟶ I used to ask the kids to decorate the table; they're always full of creative ideas. Now they're older (and have other things to do), so I make do by myself and cover the table with candles. I spread a colored tablecloth (navy blue always makes a good impression) and I get out my enamel tableware (as you've probably realized, it's my passion) and my matte gold cutlery. I try to pick two or three flowers or repurpose a bouquet and arrange in mini vases on the table.

30 minutes to go

⟶ I used to think it was important to offer an array of alcoholic pre-dinner drinks. But actually, if you have red wine and white wine, that's enough; everyone will be happy. And you'll make it through the evening. For those who don't drink alcohol, provide water and juice, and that's all there is to it. Oh, and don't forget the ginger beer— *Parisiennes* are addicted to this drink right now.

They're here

⟶ When the guests arrive, I offer them sesame breadsticks served in a glass (for a decorative touch), a few pretzels, and some cherry tomatoes and baby veggies (also served in a glass). The goal is to keep your guests hungry before sitting down to dinner. I've noticed that the longer they have to wait, the more delicious they'll find your meal.

1 ½ hours later

⟶ It's time to cook the basmati rice—always an elegant touch. By now, your guests' tummies are rumbling and they're growing impatient.

2 hours later

⟶ Your guests are starving; they devour their meal. And they love the chicken: "What's in this again?" I've realized something over the years: people don't come over to eat. They come to see you, not for a gourmet meal. There are enough chefs out there providing that already. You don't have to prove you're a Cordon Bleu master. At one of the best dinners I was invited to recently, the host asked everyone, "What do you want on your pizza?"

Then he ordered from the Italian restaurant down the street. He has it figured out: we were delighted with our meal, and he was able to spend a nice evening with us. It's rather passé to spend your night slaving over a hot stove. If you do insist on moonlighting as Ducasse, prepare as much as possible ahead of time.

After 3 hours

⟶ Always surprise your guests with something amusing for dessert. I like serving chocolate mousse in miniature aluminum pots; it's like having a dolls' tea party. Or, if I serve a good ice cream—which I buy, of course—I scoop it into waffle cones. It's so much nicer like that! In the end, just as in fashion and design, less is more. By not overdoing things, you'll be sure to create a relaxed ambiance. I'll bet that hordes of women chained to the old-fashioned rules for entertaining will quickly convert to this method—it's much more fun than stuffy old dinners.

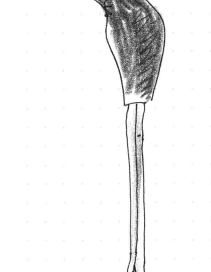

apps in Paris

Besides hosting a dinner when I'm in Paris, my first instinct when I'm hungry is to pick up my telephone and order a meal. With home delivery services like Deliveroo I can "let go" and shake off the constraints of making dinner. I usually order from Wild & The Moon, one of the healthiest restaurants I know. My favorite drink is the Black Gold, which contains almonds, charcoal, dates, vanilla, and sea salt. Ok, it sounds weird, but I'm telling you, it's very good.

French diet

I often get asked what diet I follow. Everyone would like to crack the *Parisienne*'s secret and learn how she maintains her figure. I can tell you that as far as I'm concerned, I never follow diets. However, there's one golden rule that governs my eating habits: I pay attention when I'm eating and stop when I'm no longer hungry.

DECO ADDRESSES

The Socialite Family

✳ Constance Gennari, founder and artistic director of The Socialite Family, is a self-proclaimed fan of the new generation of parents. With them in mind, she creates timeless but modern furniture. Her business model also meets contemporary demands: to guarantee a fair price, The Socialite Family cuts out the middleman.

12, rue Saint-Fiacre, 2ᵉ
Tel. +33 (0)1 82 28 06 60
thesocialitefamily.com
International delivery available

Maison de Vacances

I'd barely got through the door and already I wanted my house to look exactly like this place. The owners— a former designer and a former art director—are lovely people. They commission some objects, buy others, and throw in a few unique vintage pieces. I love the linen sheets in refined colors, quilted napkins, wooden objects, ceramics, lamps, and hanging light fixtures. The slogan at this Bohemian-chic boutique is "Dress your home as you would yourself."

4, rue de Cléry, 2ᵉ
Tel. +33 (0)1 42 86 94 69
maisondevacances.com
International delivery available

Borgo delle Tovaglie

✱ The lavish decor in this 7,500-square-foot (700 m²) concept store is a blend of industrial chic and Italian *dolce vita*. Wicker baskets, household linen, old-fashioned dishware—I want it all. To calm my urge to buy the entire store, I enjoy a plate of homemade pasta in the small Italian bistro, which you can also hire for private parties. You won't ever want to leave.

4, rue du Grand-Prieuré, 11ᵉ
Tel. +33 (0)9 82 33 64 81
borgodelletovaglie.com
International delivery available

AMPM

✳ Until now, this interior design catalog, adored by *Parisiennes*, didn't have a physical store to showcase products. Now you'll find the brand's showrooms in Paris, where certain items are available for purchase, while others must be ordered. I often buy their linen sheets online, but it's nice to be able to see the colors before ordering. The same goes for curtains; it's reassuring to see what they look like in real life. My favorite curtains are also linen, but sometimes I improvise using simple bedsheets attached to black clip rings. I like to change cutlery often; it makes each dinner unique. AMPM sells black and gold varieties. You could even mix them together to create surprising new place settings. This is also where I find my display boxes that I use everywhere, from the kitchen to my closet.

62, rue de Bonaparte, 6ᵉ
ampm.fr
International delivery available

Astier de Villatte

✳ This is my favorite tableware store. It's both refined and minimalist. I like to display little ceramic pieces around my house like works of art. Astier de Villatte also stocks incense, scented candles (I have a soft spot for one called "Le Grand Chalet," named after a charming place in Switzerland), as well as creations that are both chic and amusing, like a porcelain tureen with Snoopy on the lid—that'll get the kids to eat their soup!

16, rue de Tournon, 6ᵉ
Tel. +33 (0)1 42 03 43 90
astierdevillatte.com
European delivery available
Available in the USA at John Derian:
johnderian.com/collections/astier-de-villatte

Mint & Lilies

✳ Everything here is charming, fresh, poetic, and affordable. Our kind of place, right? This is a truly appealing interior design store. You'll find lots of objects in pleasing materials: I've found fluted glasses, glass jars with gold stoppers, and even elegant brushes, not to mention pretty Indian jewelry.

27–29, rue Daguerre, 14ᵉ
Tel. +33 (0)1 43 35 30 25
mintandlilies.com
International delivery available

Les Fleurs

✳ Contrary to what its name suggests, this store doesn't sell flowers; instead you'll find decorative objects, small leather goods, jewelry, scarves, and stationery. You might say it's a touch "Bobo," since people like to identify stores by style. But its real charm lies in the vintage furniture scattered around. Just try to leave empty-handed.

6, passage Josset, 11ᵉ
5, rue Trousseau, 11ᵉ
boutiquelesfleurs.com
International delivery available

Rivières

✱ I discovered this boutique the last time I moved house. Everything here looks like it's been brought back from a trip abroad. Black and white dominate the reigning ethnic-chic style. Carpets, wooden spoons, metal dishware, baskets (the black enamel coffeepots deserve a mention)—it has everything I love. The traveling adventurers who opened this shop are always picking up things from far-flung places. But the store is only open on Saturday.

15, rue Saint-Yves, 14ᵉ
Open Saturday from 11 a.m. to 7 p.m.
rivieres-rivieres.com
International delivery available

Saint-Ouen Flea Market

✱ Everyone heads to the Paul Bert section, but I like to change things up and head to the Vernaison section. That's where you'll find Tombées du Camion (99, rue des Rosiers, 93400 Saint-Ouen, tombeesducamion.com). It's a treasure trove of delightful antique objects in perfect condition. The owner has a talent for creating whimsical displays. You're as likely to find a whistle here as you are an egg cup, old medicine tins, a chalkboard, notepaper, plates, bottles, toys steeped in nostalgia, or old-fashioned packaging. My favorites? Makeup and medicine tins with amazing labels. Don't leave me alone for too long in this place, because I am fully capable of buying up the entire stock. In my shopping basket you'll find salt shakers, dishes, tiny tea-party platters, Porto glasses, mini bottles that will serve as vases for individual flowers, a tape measure. This Aladdin's cave of wonders is chockablock full of forgotten vintage gadgets that suddenly seem absolutely essential.

Merci

Marie-France Cohen, who founded childrenswear brand Bonpoint, is a visionary and realized ten years ago that a store with a sustainable attitude was just the thing for the twenty-first century. And so Merci was born. A portion of the store's profits go to funding education and development projects in southwest Madagascar. She has since sold the store, but the 16,000-square-foot (1500 m²) space still stocks high-end objects (including furniture) as well as everyday wares, like household linen and clever designer kitchen accessories. The clothing and jewelry is created exclusively for Merci, along with pencils in a rainbow of colors and vintage-style notebooks. You'll find a little bit of everything here, but most of the brands are carefully chosen and have an ethical element. It's the kind of pretty jumble we love. We say "merci, Merci!"

111, boulevard Beaumarchais, 3ᵉ
Tel. +33 (0)1 42 77 00 33
merci-merci.com/en
International delivery available

Bookbinders Design

✳ A black photo album inscribed in silver lettering with a name or a year is decidedly chic. The brand has gone green with its 100-percent recycled notebooks.

130, rue du Bac, 7ᵉ
Tel. +33 (0)1 42 22 73 66
Locations worldwide
bookbindersdesign.com/en
International delivery available

World Style

✳ Ok, so radiators have never really drawn a crowd. But Parisians flock to see these because they're all so stylish. This is an address worth noting: designer radiators are hard to come by, after all.

25, rue de Cléry, 2ᵉ
Tel. +33 (0)1 40 26 92 69
worldstyle.com
International delivery available upon request

Vincent Darré

✳ Vincent Darré is one of my favorite designers. He worked in fashion before venturing into the field of art furnishings. He is extremely creative: his objects and furniture combine precision and spirit, like the Libellule lamp and the Centaure table— irresistible and amusing.

13, rue Royale, 8ᵉ
By appointment only
Tel. +33 (0)1 40 07 95 62
maisondarre.com

PARIS · EXCLUSIVE

Caravane

✳ Caravane has impeccably designed sofas and a host of other furniture and ornaments that will make you an instant fan of its contemporary-exotic-Parisian style. The furniture displays are all incredibly refined. Visit the store, gather inspiration, and then recreate it at home. I never get tired of the superb fabrics you can use to drape over sofas. What's Caravane's bestseller? The Thala sofa with a removeable cover. Once you sit down in it, you'll never want to get up. An enchanting, cosmopolitan, urban, and oh-so-Parisian place—though Caravane now has outposts in many French cities, as well as London and Copenhagen.

9 and 16, rue Jacob, 6ᵉ. 19 and 22, rue Saint-Nicolas, 12ᵉ. London: Units 52/54, Coal Drops Yard, Stable Street, N1C 4DQ; 38/40 New Cavendish Street, W1G 8UD
caravane.co.uk
International delivery available

Eric Philippe

 Located in one of the most beautiful covered passages in Paris, this store specializes in twentieth-century furniture, notably Scandinavian designs from 1920 to 1980. You'll also find 1950s American designers. Pure, beautiful—just my style.

25, galerie Véro-Dodat, 1er
Tel. +33 (0)1 42 33 28 26
ericphilippe.com

Gypel

This frame maker can show any object, photo, or painting to its best advantage. He's full of great ideas and can do whatever you ask for. A must-visit.

9, rue Jean-Jacques Rousseau, 1er
Tel. +33 (0)1 42 36 15 79

Galerie du Passage

Just opposite Eric Philippe's gallery is one run by Pierre Passebon, known the world over for his incredible selection of furniture and objects from the twentieth century to the present day. The gallery always seems to be hosting a detour-worthy exhibition. We'll see if you can make it out of this welcoming space without falling for one of the many desirable objects on display.

20–26, galerie Véro-Dodat, 1er
Tel. +33 (0)1 42 36 01 13
galeriedupassage.com

e-deco

selency.fr

✳ My favorite site—I can spend hours browsing the well-organized categories. I always find something incredible. It's a little like Vestiaire Collective (see p. 121), only you buy and sell furniture instead of clothes. Some people visit just for inspiration. But I have a hard time believing they aren't tempted to click on a few of the wonderful pieces they see. The best section to explore is the "Top 200 Items to Bid On."

dexam.co.uk

✳ This English company founded in 1957 specializes in kitchen utensils. You'll also find enameled dishware—Dexam Vintage—which I'm not ashamed to admit I collect.

avidaportuguesa.com

✳ The website of a Portuguese brand with four stores in Lisbon. Bring a little sunshine into your home.

cosydar-deco.com

✳ You'll only find objects in natural, untreated materials on this website. The clothes rack in wrought iron and laurel wood is so beautiful you can display it like a work of art.

madeindesign.com

✳ The number one online design website. My first stop is the "Clearance" section, which always has good deals. Then I click on the "Inspiration" tab because it's full of great ideas. Parisiennes order Luxembourg chairs by Fermob to bring a little of the famous Parisian garden into their home.

Exclusively français

onrangetout.com

✳ Organization is another of my passions, and this French website is my guiding light. It's very thorough, and everything is organized by space: living room, bathroom, basement, etc. If you're looking for ideas to organize your closet, this is the place to go—you'll find the solution to any problem.

decoclico.fr

✳ An exhaustive decoration site in French that I like particularly for its kitchen section, where you'll find lots of storage suggestions.

lovecreativepeople.com

✳ Every brand on this French site— selected from around the world— is worth knowing about. All the everyday objects, like coffee pots and cooking utensils, have a little extra character. That's rare these days, which makes this place remarkable.

madeleine-gustave.com

✳ Once located near the Canal Saint-Martin, this store is currently searching for a new home in Paris. In the meantime, head to the French website, where everything inspires me. I raided the former store: a copper tray, a saucer for holding bathroom soap, metal towel racks, porcelain ladles and spoons, wooden bowls, and enameled objects (I never get tired of those). The owner must be a Leo with Gemini rising because I want everything she picks out.

Flower power

You'll find a florist on every corner, but not many of them are creative enough to make bouquets with a wow factor. Here are my top five in Paris.

Arôm Paris

✱ Incredibly imaginative bouquets. The store often creates the decor for fashionable evening events.

73, avenue Ledru-Rollin, 12ᵉ
Tel. +33 (0)1 43 46 82 59
aromparis.fr

Thalie

✱ A bouquet is like a fine meal: you need good ingredients and a good chef. And that's what you'll find in Pascale Leray at Thalie, who only uses the highest quality flowers. She has things you won't find anywhere else (like cherry tree branches) and she hosts workshops where you can learn to compose your own bouquets.

223, rue Saint-Jacques, 5ᵉ
Tel. +33 (0)1 43 54 41 00

Florists

Lachaume

✱ This store reflects the high fashion spirit of the sophisticated bouquets crafted by this master florist since 1845. I'm partial to the house candle, with its notes of violet (my daughter's name is Violette). When you're after something a bit more unusual, order the bouquet of 250 ears of golden wheat.

103, rue du Faubourg Saint-Honoré, 8ᵉ
Tel. +33 (0)1 42 60 59 74
maisonlachaume.com
International delivery available

Eric Chauvin

✱ A French master of the art of flower arranging, this florist creates romantic bouquets. His compositions with white flowers are sublime.

22, rue Jean-Nicot, 7ᵉ
Tel. +33 (0)1 45 50 43 54
ericchauvin.fr/en

Moulié

✱ Upholding French traditions since 1870, Moulié is known for supplying ministries, embassies, and haute-couture designers. The bouquets come at a price, of course, but the result is always breathtaking.

8, place du Palais-Bourbon, 7ᵉ
Tel. +33 (0)1 45 51 78 43
mouliefleurs.com

FRENCHY GIFT IDEAS

What gift should you offer to prove you're a real Frenchy? Here are five ideas.

FOR A PARISIAN DINNER: Cire Trudon or Diptyque

✸ When you're invited to a dinner party, a candle is an ideal gift because you can bring it with you to work and go directly from the office to dinner (flowers are harder to manage). The *Parisienne* is always torn between Cire Trudon and Diptyque. The first has been around since 1634 and supplied the royal court. The latter appeared more recently (the first candle was created in 1963) and is very modern—it invented one of the first unisex eaux de toilette. Make sure you smell L'Admirable by Cire Trudon and Feu de Bois by Diptyque.

Cire Trudon: 78, rue de Seine, 6ᵉ
Tel. +33 (0)1 43 26 46 50
ciretrudon.com
Diptyque: 34, boulevard Saint-Germain, 5ᵉ
Tel. +33 (0)1 43 26 77 44
diptyqueparis.com

FOR A FOODIE: Confiture Parisienne

✸ "Some jam is meant to be spread, other jam is meant to be eaten with a spoon." The little jars by Confiture Parisienne fall into the second category. The unique recipes are developed by chefs, so you could call this haute cuisine. Make sure you taste the fruit butter made with coconut oil and various fruits. For a really sophisticated gift, have the jar personalized.

17, avenue Daumesnil, 12ᵉ
Tel. +33 (0)1 44 68 28 81
confiture-parisienne.com

FOR A JAPAN ENTHUSIAST: Bows and Arrows

✈ True *Parisiennes* love all things Japanese, and this Parisian store, specializing in the finest design Japan has to offer, is a veritable window onto the best of the Japanese art of living. Most people think of traveling to Japan for kimonos and fans, but I come here for all the different gadgets, from notebooks to pens to copper teapots.

17, rue Notre-Dame-de-Nazareth, 3ᵉ
bows-and-arrows.net
International delivery available

FOR A FRANCOPHILE: boutique.elysee.fr

✈ The Elysée website, the official store of the presidential residence, sells products that proclaim our love for France. With bags emblazoned with *Première Dame* (First Lady) and bracelets declaring *Liberté* (Liberty) by Atelier Paulin, this is the Frenchiest online gift shop that exists (for the moment). And it serves a purpose: all profits go to restoring the 300-year-old Élysée Palace.

boutique.elysee.fr
International delivery available

FOR A CREATIVE SPIRIT: Adam or Sennelier

✈ Here, you'll find everything you need to draw. Adam has been selling art supplies since 1898, and Sennelier since 1887. A few famous masters like Modigliani were known to stock up at these art stores. I love the papers, pencils, paints, and all the colors.

Adam: 11, boulevard Edgar-Quinet, 14ᵉ
Tel. +33 (0)1 43 20 68 53
adamparis.com
Sennelier: 3, quai Voltaire, 7ᵉ
Tel. +33 (0)1 42 60 72 15
magasinsennelier.net

ONLY IN PARIS

Musée
Jacquemart-
André

PARISIAN STROLLS

When Parisians are finished shopping
and dining, what else do they like to do?
Here's what residents of the City of Light
do in their spare time.

Visit unusual museums

Of course there's the Louvre, the Musée d'Orsay, and Beaubourg, but locals prefer visiting less prominent museums. Here are 7 of my favorite museums.

Musée Jacquemart-André

✳ A collection of Flemish and Italian Renaissance paintings amid rare furniture. The café-tea room is one of the most charming in the capital.

158, boulevard Haussmann, 8ᵉ
Tel. +33 (0)1 45 62 11 59
musee-jacquemart-andre.com/en/home

Musée Marmottan Monet

✳ This Impressionist museum is located in a pretty *hôtel particulier* with a garden. Here, you can admire the world's largest collection of works by Claude Monet. Now that's impressive!

2, rue Louis-Boilly, 16ᵉ
Tel. +33 (0)1 44 96 50 33
marmottan.fr/en

Musée d'Art Moderne de la Ville de Paris

✳ Following its remodel in late 2019, the MAM with its contemporary art collection—including over thirteen thousand twentieth- and twenty-first-century works—is the city's hottest museum.

12–14, avenue de New York, 16ᵉ
Tel. +33 (0)1 53 67 40 00
mam.paris.fr/en

Musée de la Vie Romantique

✳ A charming place where you can easily imagine George Sand or Chopin waltzing in at any moment. The lovely garden would make the perfect setting for a marriage proposal.

16, rue Chaptal, 9ᵉ
Tel. +33 (0)1 55 31 95 67
museevieromantique.paris.fr/en

Musée Cognacq-Jay

 This small art museum is a well-kept secret—even in Paris! You'll find eighteenth-century paintings, sculptures, drawings, furniture, and porcelain, all of it collected by Ernest Cognacq, founder of the Parisian department store La Samaritaine. Very Paris, indeed.

8, rue Elzévir, 3ᵉ
Tel. +33 (0)1 40 27 07 21
museecognacqjay.paris.fr/en

Musée Delacroix

 I held my book launch for *The Parisian Field Guide to Men's Style* in the garden of this museum. Surprisingly, it's smack in the middle of the 6ᵉ *arrondissement*. Place de Fürstenburg, without a doubt, is one of the most charming squares in Paris. If you like Eugène Delacroix's work, this museum shouldn't be missed.

6, rue de Fürstenberg, 6ᵉ
Tel. +33 (0)1 44 41 86 50
musee-delacroix.fr/en

Musée Bourdelle

This place exudes old-time Montparnasse. Bourdelle's sculpture workshop is fully intact and the temporary exhibitions are always interesting. The garden is an ideal spot for a relaxed tête-à-tête.

18, rue Antoine Bourdelle, 15ᵉ
Tel. +33 (0)1 49 54 73 73
bourdelle.paris.fr/en

Hang out in English bookstores

Galignani

✈ This was the first English bookstore to open on the continent. Today you'll find more than just English-language books; the fashion section is amazing—I could spend hours browsing!

224, rue de Rivoli, 1ᵉʳ
Tel. +33 (0)1 42 60 76 07
galignani.com

WH Smith

✈ This store is a hot spot for English-language magazines. You'll find me there just before Christmas, looking for typically British presents and children's books (the selection is fantastic!). And, I'll admit, also for the English chocolates you can't find anywhere else in Paris.

48, rue de Rivoli, 1ᵉʳ
Tel. +33 (0)1 44 77 88 99
whsmith.fr

WANDER AROUND SAINT-GERMAIN-DES-PRÉS

Although I now live in the 14ᵉ *arrondissement*, whenever I have a minute I head to the 6ᵉ. Besides exploring the neighborhood's many shops, I particularly enjoy these three spots:

→ **Cour de Rohan.** The courtyard is closed on the weekend, but open to the public during the week. Formerly named Cour de Rouen (perhaps because it was inhabited by bishops from Rouen), it's unique in Paris. You can't shop here; just take in the beauty.

→ **Church of Saint-Germain-des-Prés.** This is the oldest church in Paris. If you stand on the sidewalk facing the church, in front of the restaurant La Société, you can snap a picture that will score you lots of "likes" on Instagram.

→ **Place de l'Odéon.** This is what is known as the perfect movie location. It looks like it's straight out of a theater stage set. If you manage to make your way onto the theater terrace, you'll be treated to a wonderful view of the Paris rooftops.

PARIS FOR KIDS

My friends who live outside of Paris always ask me,
"How do you manage with kids in the city?"
It's very easy: Paris has so many ways to keep them
occupied, I've never even asked myself the question.
Museums, parks, toy stores, bookshops, shows,
and monuments—in Paris, a day out with the kids
is always fun.

For a budding chef

Chez Bogato

✳ You can order impressive birthday cakes here—and when you do, don't feel bad about grabbing one of the single-serving pastries for yourself. They also offer workshops for aspiring pastry chefs (for kids, parents + kids, or adults). Invite your child's friends to a birthday party at a pastry shop (4 years and up): it's a good warm-up before auditioning for a television cooking show.

7, rue Liancourt, 14ᵉ
Tel. +33 (0)1 40 47 03 51
chezbogato.fr

École Ritz-Escoffier

✳ What's the best gift you could give a kid who wants to be Rémy the rat from *Ratatouille*? Cooking lessons at Ritz-Escoffier in the kitchen of the Hôtel Ritz. The little chefs (6 to 11 years old, accompanied by a parent) get to don a real chef's uniform and prepare a dish of their choice from the program's website. They'll be begging to come back!

15, place Vendôme, 1ᵉʳ
Tel. +33 (0)1 43 16 30 50
ritzescoffier.com/en-GB

LE BON MARCHÉ

The department store recently redesigned its children's section, which is one of the chicest in the capital. You're sure to find something you like from among the mix of classic and on-trend brands. The bonus? Wednesday, Saturday, and Sunday, you can take advantage of two hours of childcare while you go shopping. The challenge is to remember to pick up your kids once you're done. Reservations at Planyo.com.

How are little Parisians made?

Confined in their city, Parisians sorely lack greenery. But when it comes to activities, they're the lucky ones. Between museums, creative visits to the city, and workshops, they have a multitude of entertainment options at their fingertips.

Parisdenfants.com

→ For Francophones, only: creative museum visits or outings (including treasure hunts) in Paris, for kids 5 years and up. They're so much fun, you'll never hear your kids say, "When are we leaving the museum?" or "I can't walk anymore. I want to take the metro!"

Where can I find a workshop?

→ If you don't have kids, it's not easy to figure out how to keep them busy, should you decide to play Mary Poppins for a day. This French-only website has you covered: **atelierenfant.com**, which offers workshops organized by neighborhood and age. It also offers workshops for birthday parties. In a word, it's supercalifragilisticexpialidocious!

Learn at the museum

→ Some museums have specially trained guides to captivate children. At the Louvre, you can download a selection of interesting guided itineraries before you go (louvre.fr/en/parcours). The Musée d'Orsay has a website for kids where you can sign up for workshops in French (petitsmo.fr). Every weekend and during school holidays, the Fondation Louis Vuitton organizes fifteen-minute storytelling visits for children from 3 to 5 years old (accompanied by a parent) and workshops for kids from 6 to 10 years old: fondationlouisvuitton.fr/en/calendar.html.

**✳ The cafeteria
at the Musée Rodin**

In summer, this is the best place to
have lunch with your kids: they'll be
surrounded by lush vegetation as well
as famous sculptures. Educating
oneself without seeming to try is
the sign of a budding Parisian.

79, rue de Varenne, 7ᵉ
Tel. +33 (0)1 44 18 61 10
musee-rodin.fr/en

**✳ Muséum National d'Histoire
Naturelle & Ménagerie du Jardin
des Plantes**

Every Parisian child has come to this
natural history museum at least once
(often with his or her school) to admire
the Gallery of Evolution and all the
stuffed animals and taxidermy. In good
weather, head to the *ménagerie*, one of
the oldest zoos in Europe. Thousands
of parents have experienced the drama
of trying to pull a child away from the
monkeys as the zoo is closing. Don't
miss the four tropical greenhouses.

36, rue Geoffroy Saint-Hilaire, 5ᵉ
Tel. +33 (0)1 40 79 54 79
mnhn.fr/en

✳ Palais de Tokyo

This contemporary museum doesn't
have a permanent collection, but the
exhibitions are always very interesting.
If you have kids, check out the Tok-Tok
workshops (palaisdetokyo.com/en/
event/tok-tok-workshops). Kids get
to visit the exhibition and create
their own works related to the world
they discover.

13, avenue du Président Wilson, 15ᵉ
Tel. +33 (0)1 47 23 54 01
palaisdetokyo.com/en

For a breath of fresh air

Jardin du Luxembourg

✱ Kids on the Left Bank love the Luxembourg Gardens. It's a shame there's only a tiny strip of grass open for picnicking. But luckily there are lots of other things to do. Here's the perfect afternoon outing to ensure your kids hit the hay early:

→ Begin at the fountain outside the Sénat building: rent a little sail boat that your child can push along with a stick. Watch the ducks.

→ Head to the swings (next to the tennis courts). Put your child in a swing and push.

→ Every effort deserves a reward. It's time for a crêpe in the bar next to the puppet theater. Or have a delicious lunch on the terrace of La Table du Luxembourg next door.

→ Let the show begin (especially if it's raining and it's the middle of winter) at the covered theater: your kids will remember the Marionnettes de Luxembourg, an old-fashioned puppet show, for the rest of their lives.

→ Take a whirl on the merry-go-round outside the theater to get them back in the saddle. But they won't just sit there: with a little stick, they have to snatch iron rings from the "merry-go-round man."

→ Finish on a high note with a pony ride (on the path facing the Guynemer entrance). After all that, you're guaranteed to have a peaceful evening. Unless you're also worn out after such an exciting day!

Jardin des Tuileries

✱ If your kids are the kind to jump on the bed when they don't know what to do, take them to this garden, where eight large trampolines await. That's even more fun than riding a merry-go-round!

Parc des Buttes Chaumont

✳ It's a bit of a haul for me to get to the 19ᵉ *arrondissement* from the 14ᵉ, but this rolling park has some of the best views of Paris. Like the Luxembourg Gardens, this park has games, a puppet theater, and ponies. What do kids really love here? The stalactite-filled caves, the waterfall, the footbridge, and the hanging bridge. Even better, you can picnic on the grass. That's definitely worth the metro fare!

Jardin Catherine Labouré

✳ This garden is hidden away from view behind stone walls. It's one of the few gardens in Paris where you're allowed to walk on the grass. For a chic picnic, grab some provisions at the Grande Épicerie nearby. No one who comes here does so by accident.

29, rue de Babylone, 7ᵉ

Eiffel Tower

✳ Impossible to avoid! To skip the lines of tourists, buy your tickets online (toureiffel.paris/en) or walk up!

For animal lovers

The Paris Zoo

✳ With around 180 species and over 200 animals, this is a well-stocked zoo. Get ready for a trip around the world, from Africa to Patagonia. Sign up ahead of time for onsite workshops— animal caretakers in training, for example. Take note: you can also download activity books for your visit.

At the intersection of avenue Daumesnil and route de la Ceinture du Lac, 12ᵉ parczoologiquedeparis.fr/en

---

Shopping for kids

Smallable

✳ It's impossible not to walk out with something from this family concept store (fashion, design, toys) that's been showcasing the most fashionable selection for babies and kids for ten years now. Good taste assured. It's also a great place to find baby shower gifts. One of my favorites is Numéro 74, a Spanish brand created by two cousins, one Italian and the other French—even that piqued my interest. When I learned that the products are handmade by members of a self-run women's community in Thailand, I was hooked. Everything in the store is made of organic cotton, from dresses to backpacks. There's even a women's collection. I could write a whole book on this store! The brand recently opened a small shop across the street for newborns and babies.

81–82, rue du Cherche-Midi, 6ᵉ
Tel. +33 (0)1 40 46 01 15
en.smallable.com
International delivery available

WOMB

✳ WOMB (World of My Baby) is the perfect concept store for parents. Located in the heart of the Sentier district, it sells everything you need to welcome a new baby (strollers, sleep sacks, and even wallpaper), as well as clothes and toys by fun brands (Arsène et les Pipelettes, Jojo Factory, Emile et Ida). You can also create a baby registry (also available online).

93, rue de Réaumur, 2ᵉ
Tel. +33 (0)1 42 36 36 37
wombconcept.com
International delivery available

Bonpoint

✈ No one leaves Bonpoint empty-handed! Especially not the beautiful boutique on rue de Tournon. Babies, little girls, and little boys—the style is the same for everyone: nothing but good taste in subtle colors, delicate prints (the famous Liberty print!), and "easy chic" cuts. Go for the down jackets in winter and the embroidered dresses or boys' shirts in summer. The perfume for babies makes a great shower gift (every mom nabs this from their little one). In the garden you'll find the restaurant La Guinguette d'Angèle, where everything is very healthy, so highly recommended.

6, rue de Tournon, 6ᵉ
Tel. +33 (0)1 40 51 98 20
Locations worldwide
bonpoint.com/us or /gb
International delivery available

Louis Louise

✳ The collections by Louis Louise, with their Bohemian-chic style and ethnic prints, are deliriously charming. The creators make cute dresses minus the schmaltz. This kind of store makes me nostalgic for the days when my girls were little.

83, rue du Cherche-Midi, 6ᵉ
63, rue de Turenne, 3ᵉ
Tel. +33 (0)9 80 63 85 95
louislouise.com/en
International delivery available

Pom d'Api

✳ With over a century of experience, this creator has been making shoes for children in France and around the world since 1870. When you want a pair of quality shoes for your baby's first steps, head to this store. The Plagette is the star of sandals, a must-have for budding Parisians. New models are released each season, and Pom d'Api also proposes the brand Collection Originale, which lets you customize shoes with interchangeable accessories—perfectly in line with the "I made it myself!" trend.

Baudou

✳ Although the name has changed, this store still sells Bonpoint furniture. It's the perfect place to shop for a kid's room if you can't stand kitsch: the colors are soft and there are no useless embellishments. It's the perfect place to find a simple straw bassinet, a minimalist bedframe, and even a polar bear lamp. And if you don't have any more room for furniture, get a stuffed animal—they're all irresistible.

13, rue du Jour, 1ᵉʳ
Tel. +33 (0)1 42 36 08 87
28, rue du Four, 6ᵉ
Tel. +33 (0)1 45 48 39 31
Locations worldwide
pomdapi.fr/en
European delivery available

7, rue de Solferino, 7ᵉ
Tel. +33 (0)1 45 55 42 79
baudoumeuble.com
International delivery available

Fashion kid

3 ideas for dressing the little ones:

→ Avoid combining loud prints: they're children, not clowns.

→ Don't hesitate to dress them in head-to-toe black—it'll get dirty less easily. If you want a cheerier look, add a colorful pair of shoes, scarf, or coat. And you don't have to be under 10 to steal this style tip!

→ To prevent your kids from leading a fashion riot, regularly let them pick out an item of clothing. Too bad if your son absolutely insists on that neon orange shirt with his favorite superhero or your daughter demands a pink tutu. We've all made youthful errors!

Bonton

✱ If you're looking for simple, easy-to-wear clothes for your kids, this is the place to go. How do they do it? With a touch of bobo style, beautiful materials, and bright—but not flashy—colors. In the first edition of this book, we said we'd like to see Bonton collections in adult sizes. We got our wish: there's now a women's collection. Kids will find lots of fun things to decorate their room in this concept store. The Bonton boutique in the 3ᵉ *arrondissement* even has a *capilliculteur*—a hairdresser—for kids (appointments online).

5, boulevard des Filles-du-Calvaire, 3ᵉ
Tel. +33 (0)1 42 72 34 69
82, rue de Grenelle, 7ᵉ
Tel. +33 (0)1 44 39 09 20
bonton.fr/en_us or /en_uk
International delivery available

IE

✱ *Ie* is a Japanese word that means "house." When this store first opened, it specialized in homewares but the focus has since changed, and now it stocks an in-house collection of clothing (newborn to 8 years). The designs are beautiful and everything is produced in India from natural, artisan-woven and -printed materials. Supremely sustainable! You'll find beautiful, unique fabrics in the store and on the brand's website (you can buy them by the yard/meter). You'll also find a wide selection of objects from India, Japan, and elsewhere around the world.

128, rue Vieille-du-Temple, 3ᵉ
Tel. +33 (0)1 44 59 87 72
ieboutique.com
International delivery available

Bass

✱ Stores with wood or cast-iron toys always have good energy. The wooden toys at Bass are new but inspired by retro toys—old-fashioned style is wildly popular in the age of video games. The metal wind-up toys are charming, especially the robot and the elephant.

8, rue de l'Abbé-de-l'Epée, 5ᵉ
Tel. +33 (0)1 43 25 97 01
bass-paris.com
International delivery available

La Mouette Rieuse

✳ Step into this cultural concept store filled with books and you'll realize right away that you'll be staying for a while. Books about Paris line the entrance (from guides to the best restaurants in the city to volumes replete with photographs by Henri Cartier-Bresson). The first-floor bookstore is dedicated to children's books, with an adorably cute collection by hard-to-find publishers. And if you need a break, there's a café with a little courtyard at the back of the store.

17 bis, rue Pavée, 4ᵉ
Tel. +33 (0)1 43 70 34 74

Le Petit Souk

✳ When you need a baby shower gift, this is the place to go for amusing objects and clothes that aren't too kitsch, like the rabbit-shaped nightlight and the sleep sacks in fun fabrics. You'll also find decorative objects and stationery supplies—you can never have too many notebooks!

17, rue Vavin, 6ᵉ
Tel. +33 (0)1 42 02 23 71
lepetitsouk.fr

Chantelivre

✳ The window displays at this shrine to children's books are always bursting with ideas. A bookstore that makes every child want to read is quite an achievement. Plus the staff members at Chantelivre can summarize any book you like and tell you what kind of reader will enjoy it. There's also an adult section with the latest titles—hey, did you buy my book here?

13, rue de Sèvres, 6ᵉ
Tel. +33 (0)1 45 48 87 90
chantelivre.fr
International delivery available

Milk on the Rocks

✳ Unique details, rock-and-roll prints, surprising colors, and comfortable materials: parents like the clothes at Milk on the Rocks, but so do kids. And you can take them shopping with you because there are lots of little gadgets in the store to keep them busy.

7, rue de Mézières, 6ᵉ
Tel. +33 (0)1 45 49 19 84
Locations worldwide
milkontherocks.net
International delivery available

Agnès b. Enfants

✳ This is the perfect brand if you want to dress your kid in black. Agnès b. was one of the first designers to dare the unthinkable—I applaud her style!

2, rue du Jour, 1ᵉʳ
Tel. +33 (0)1 40 13 91 27
Locations worldwide
agnesb.fr
International delivery available

Pain d'Épices

✳ A unique store in an atmospheric covered passageway. This traditional toy store is a paradise for dolls' houses: they come in all sizes and you'll find everything to furnish them—toilets, cakes, and even miniature Monopoly boards. When I want to offer a very personal gift, I buy wood display cases to enclose objects that characterize the person: a drill if he tinkers, a doll's dress if she's a fashionista. It makes for an amusing decorative piece.

29–33, passage Jouffroy, 9ᵉ
Tel. +33 (0)1 47 70 08 68
paindepices.fr
International delivery available

Finger in the Nose

Printed T-shirts, jeans, soft sweatshirts, down jackets, and parkas: Finger in the Nose reinterprets wardrobe basics for kids in a cool, funky style.

45, avenue de Trudaine, 9ᵉ
Tel. +33 (0)1 42 06 40 19
11, rue de l'Echaudé, 6ᵉ
Tel. +33 (0)9 83 01 76 75
fingerinthenose.com
International delivery available

Marie Puce

If you're looking for a little dress in a Liberty print for your baby, head here. Keep an eye out for the Minnetonka boots and Salt Water Original sandals, which aren't always easy to find.

60, rue du Cherche-Midi, 6ᵉ
Tel. +33 (0)1 45 48 30 09
mariepuce.com/en
International delivery available

Online shops for kids

ovale.com

→ For a luxurious baby shower gift, like the solid silver rattle. It works as a key chain when baby grows up.

aliceaparis.com

→ Natural materials, simple cuts, and reasonable prices: a trio I like.

maisonette.com

→ The *Parisienne* also likes to dress her kids in hard-to-find designer clothes. Her favorite stop for rare finds is Maisonnette, an online store with a cutting-edge selection and super tempting collaborations. The site also has its own brand, Maisonnette Essentials, popular with Parisians desperate for stylish yet practical children's clothes.

BON APPÉTIT!

Parisiennes are interested in more than just fashion!
Discussing life over a meal in a stylish restaurant
brings them just as much happiness as buying
a necklace by a new designer. Traditional Parisian
bistros, fashionable spots where reservations
are essential, and restaurants with a view of
the Eiffel Tower: these addresses will turn you
into a local with good taste.

Very Paris

La Poule au Pot

THE TAKEAWAY

"Beef fillet and black
forest cake—tomorrow
I'm going for a run."

Good to know

✷ This restaurant in the heart
of Les Halles, taken over by chef Jean-
François Piège, earned a Michelin
star in less than a year. It's what
we call "bourgeoise" cuisine with
all the generosity that implies.

What to order

✷ Pile your plate with frogs' legs
(so French), leg of lamb, and the
strawberry and raspberry *giboulée*
with fromage blanc sorbet.

9, rue Vauvilliers, Iᵉʳ
Tel. +33 (0)1 42 36 32 96
lapouleaupot.com

Le Cette

THE TAKEAWAY

"It's really good—
you'll be all *set!*"

Chez Georges

Good to know

✱ Nothing changes here, especially not the menu. Andouillette sausages, celeri remoulade, herring with potatoes in oil, profiteroles—it's all still there and still satisfying!

What to order

✱ The classic pavé du Mail, a cut of peppered beef served with French fries.

1, rue du Mail, 2ᵉ
Tel. +33 (0)1 42 60 07 11

THE TAKEAWAY

"Don't break out your vintage attire for dinner here—people will think you're part of the decor!"

Good to know

✱ This restaurant appeals to both women and men. The chef is Japanese, and you can taste the allusions to his native culture in his sophisticated dishes. I recently discovered this address after I moved to my new home. It's a nice bistro with just the right atmosphere: simple and good. And the owner is charming.

What to order

✱ The sophisticated mains, the fish, and the desserts—everything is exquisite! The menu changes often, so it's hard to recommend a specific dish.

7, rue Campagne-Première, 14ᵉ
Tel. +33 (0)1 43 21 05 47
lecette.fr

Chartier Montparnasse

THE TAKEAWAY

"My lunch was so reasonably priced that I can go shopping while I'm in the neighborhood."

Good to know

✷ Like Bouillon Pigalle, people come here because it's good and not at all expensive.

What to order

✷ The roast chicken and the whipped cream puff.

59, boulevard du Montparnasse, 6ᵉ
Tel. +33 (0)1 45 49 19 00
bouillon-chartier.com/en

Le Café de Flore

The atmosphere at Le Flore

✳ Le Flore is so closely associated with Paris, it's almost cliché. It's also the heart of Saint-Germain-des-Prés and a state of mind. It evokes Jean-Paul Sartre and existentialism, Françoise Sagan, Boris Vian, and Miles Davis. But above all, it embodies a French spirit: rebellious, provocateur, merry, generous, and anti-conformist. Often a meeting spot for the Left (like the bank where it's located).

The Flore paradox

→ You can find a quiet spot (especially on the second floor), BUT you'll run into a bunch of people you know.

→ It's a modern café, BUT it looks old-fashioned.

→ It's a restaurant, BUT you can also just come for coffee.

→ It's welcoming, BUT it's huge.

→ It's anti-conformist, BUT it's a classic.

→ You might run into the writer Frédéric Beigbeder (who created the literary prize Le Prix de Flore), Steven Spielberg, Diane Kruger, the singer and actress Arielle Dombasle, Sofia Coppola, or the lawyer and former minister Georges Kiejman, BUT also lots of fashion people—and me!

When to go

✳ The weekend for lunch—but it's also a good meeting point when you're not sure how big your party will be. It's good for lunch during the week with a girlfriend, or for dinner with your beau or your friends. Basically, you could live at Le Flore!

Where to sit

✳ Left of the entrance, near the cash register—where the regulars sit. Head upstairs when you want some peace and quiet and a little more light. No matter where you sit, the lady at the cash register casts a friendly eye and the waiters sashay to and fro with kindness and humor. The pleasant atmosphere is the work of general director Miroslav Siljegovic.

What to order

→ The Colette salad (with grapefruit, lettuce hearts, and avocado).

→ Scrambled eggs, perfectly cooked.

→ The Welsh Rarebit (a specialty made with cheddar cheese, beer, and toast) that fills you up—and keeps you full.

→ Le Flore (the house croque monsieur).

→ The green bean salad (it might seem basic, but the beans are perfectly crunchy).

→ The hot chocolate with a cloud of whipped cream or the *chocolat liégois*.

Dress code

✳ Respect a certain "easy chic," Left Bank elegance (jeans, a man's jacket, and ballet flats, for example). My advice: avoid red (the color of the booths), or you'll be invisible.

172, boulevard Saint-Germain, 6ᵉ
Open daily from 7 a.m. to 2 a.m.
Tel. +33 (0)1 45 48 55 26
cafedeflore.fr

Le Bon Saint Pourçain

THE TAKEAWAY

"I first learned
of this restaurant
in a James Ellroy novel."

Good to know

✈ This has always been my favorite restaurant—a typical Parisian haunt that embodies the capital. It was bought by a great guy, David Lanher, who is also behind Racines, Caffè Stern, and Noglu (a gluten-free restaurant and fine foods store). The ambiance is more cheerful now, and Mathieu Techer's food is to die for.

What to order

✳ Leeks in vinaigrette and stewed plums—well, that's if you're on a diet; otherwise there are lots of other more filling dishes to choose from.

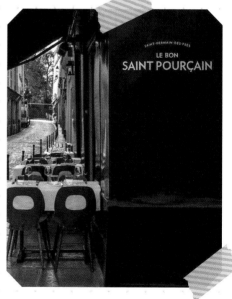

10 bis, rue Servandoni, 6ᵉ
Tel. +33 (0)1 42 01 78 24
bonsaintpourcain.com

Le Salon du Cinéma Panthéon

Good to know

✱ The first floor of one of the oldest cinemas in Paris is the best place to lunch with friends or have a cup of tea (it closes at 7 p.m.).

What to order

✱ The salads, the Iberian meat plates, organic salmon—it's all fresh and tasty.

13, rue Victor-Cousin, 6ᵉ
Tel. +33 (0)1 56 24 88 80
whynotproductions.fr/pantheon

Chez Paul

Good to know

✱ Located on the adorable place Dauphine, this restaurant is so Parisian, it could be a movie set.

What to order

✱ The sweet-and-savory duck tenders.

15, place Dauphine, 1ᵉʳ
Tel. +33 (0)1 43 54 21 48

Le Petit Lutétia

Good to know

✳ A true brasserie that draws the most elegant clientele in Paris—and I'm not just saying that because I go there, too. Ok, it might be a little noisy, but that's because the atmosphere is wonderful. The manager, Christophe, is incredibly nice. Be warned: you must reserve ahead of time, otherwise you won't be able to taste the avocado king crab or the "brasserie" tartare, both house specialties.

What to order

✳ The *putain* (*%@#!) rib steak, as it's called on the menu, and the chocolate mousse that's large enough to share.

107, rue de Sèvres, 6ᵉ
Tel. +33 (0)1 45 48 33 53

La Laiterie Sainte-Clotilde

Good to know

✳ This neighborhood restaurant draws diners from afar to sample ultra-fresh, sophisticated fare cooked up by the owner, Jean-Baptiste.

What to order

✳ The menu changes regularly. One thing is for sure: nothing is too heavy or too rich. Here you can eat well and be healthy—even the foie gras and hanger steak don't seem bad for your health. As for the pineapple with candied ginger, I'll let you be the judge.

64, rue de Bellechasse, 7ᵉ
Tel. +33 (0)1 45 51 74 61
lalaiteriesainteclotilde.fr/en

Café Verlet

THE TAKEAWAY

"This is the first restaurant to roast and serve coffee by origin."

Good to know

✴ Verlet is the oldest artisan coffee roaster in Paris still promoting French-style coffee. Connoisseurs can taste or take away over thirty varieties of coffee and forty of the world's best teas.

What to order

✴ Coffee or tea with a homemade pastry—the flaky mille-feuille, for example.

256, rue Saint-Honoré, 1er
Tel. +33 (0)1 42 60 67 39
verlet.fr/en

Bouillon Pigalle

THE TAKEAWAY

"I bought the Bouillon book, which features all its recipes. I'm going to eat the profiteroles every day."

Good to know

✱ Don't head here when you're already starving, because you can't reserve and, seeing how successful this place is (it's not expensive, given the quality), there's always a line snaking out the door. It's open every day from noon to midnight and there are 300 covers, so you're sure to make new friends.

What to order

✱ The eggs with mayonnaise, snails in parsley butter, sausages with lentils, *blanquette de veau*— it doesn't get any more French than this. For the true Bouillon experience, get the profiteroles for dessert.

22, boulevard de Clichy, 18ᵉ
Tel. +33 (0)1 42 59 69 31
bouillonpigalle.com

La Fontaine de Mars

Good to know

✳ Take advantage of the bistro's terrace in good weather.

What to order

✳ For each day of the week, there's a different dish-of-the-day. On Friday it's roasted free-range chicken and mashed potatoes. The menu also includes escargots and a very good duck breast filet. I'll only say it once: the lightly caramelized île flottante dessert is the best of its kind in the world!

129, rue Saint-Dominique, 7ᵉ
Tel. +33 (0)1 47 05 46 44
fontainedemars.com

THE TAKEAWAY

"I'm going to get the same thing Michelle Obama ate when she came here."

La Closerie des Lilas

THE TAKEAWAY

"Hemingway came here often—and so do I."

Good to know

✳ This has been *the* iconic Montparnasse restaurant since the late nineteenth century. Émile Zola, Paul Cézanne, Apollinaire, André Breton, as well Modigliani, Picasso, Jean-Paul Sartre, Oscar Wilde, and Man Ray—anyone who was anyone in the art scene came for coffee or dinner at La Closerie at some point. The restaurant side is very chic, the brasserie more approachable. That's where I head, after discussing the shellfish with the fishmonger at the entrance.

What to order

✳ The steak tartare is the house specialty—but the rest is delicious too!

171, boulevard du Montparnasse, 6ᵉ
Tel. +33 (0)1 40 51 34 50
closeriedeslilas.fr

La Calèche

Le Petit Célestin

Good to know

✳ Embodies the "Only in Paris" style. People say this spot on the quais de Seine is an old-fashioned restaurant-bistro—more importantly, it's a lovely place. In summer, a few outdoor tables complete the picture.

What to order

✳ Everything is simple and good, from the burrata with tomatoes to the tuna tartare.

12, quai des Célestins, 4ᵉ
Tel. +33 (0)1 73 20 25 24
lepetitcelestin.fr/en

Good to know

✳ This restaurant opened in 2019 in a neighborhood famous for its antiques shops. So now you know where to go for lunch or dinner when you're done shopping for furniture.

What to order

✳ Like at the Laiterie Sainte-Clotilde, also owned by Jean-Baptiste, you can confidently order whatever you want from the menu—everything is excellent. I can also tell you that the beef carpaccio draws crowds.

8, rue de Lille, 7ᵉ
Tel. +33 (0)1 40 20 94 21
lacalecheparis.fr/en

Bouillon Julien

Good to know

✳ If you're not French and you'd like to visit a restaurant that resembles what you see in the movies or the clichés about Paris, this is *the* place to reserve (you can do so online). The decor and the menu are straight out of *Ratatouille*. If you're Parisian, you must bring your foreign friends here. It's a very authentic place, and, like all *bouillons*, it's not expensive.

THE TAKEAWAY

"Édith Piaf used to come here to meet her lover, the boxer Marcel Cerdan."

What to order

✳ Everything is reasonably priced; get the "Bouillon Julien" (beef broth, fregola couscous, beef shoulder, ginger, and lemongrass), with fresh French fries, and an île flottante dessert.

16, rue du Faubourg Saint-Denis, 10ᵉ
Tel. +33 (0)1 47 70 12 06
bouillon-julien.com

And also:

Le Charlot

✴ I live on the Left Bank, so obviously I have access to many good restaurants. But when I'm in the Marais, I like this place, where the waiters are friendly and accommodating when you come with friends who are on diets and insist on eating dishes without sauce and fruit without sugar.

38, rue de Bretagne, 3ᵉ
Tel. +33 (0)1 44 54 03 30
lecharlot-paris.com

Le Select

✴ A Montparnasse institution. Perfect for a coffee in the morning or a drink later in the day. The food is very good too—don't miss the Croque Select!

99, boulevard du Montparnasse, 6ᵉ
Tel. +33 (0)1 45 48 38 24
leselectmontparnasse.fr/en

Lapérouse

✴ Everyone's talking about this recently reopened restaurant. I haven't had time to go there yet, but I have full faith in chefs Jean-Pierre Vigato and Christophe Michalak. In the nineteenth century, this restaurant was popular with Baudelaire, Zola, Maupassant, Proust, Jules Verne, and other thinkers. It still has the same muted atmosphere and private rooms where one can only guess at what once went on....

51, quai des Grands-Augustins, 6ᵉ
Tel. +33 (0)1 43 26 68 04
laperouse.com

With a view of the Eiffel Tower

Girafe

✱ Here, you'll have a front-row view of Gustave's spectacular towering masterpiece. This is an ideal place to bring foreign friends passing through Paris; they'll be impressed by the beautiful surroundings. The food is also excellent and made with exceptional ingredients. Seafood is the star, with oysters, caviar, and shellfish prepared to perfection. But there are always options for meat-eaters and vegetarians. The 1930s decor is incredibly well executed. Need I remind you? Reservations are essential.

Palais de Chaillot
1, place du Trocadéro, 16ᵉ
Tel. +33 (0)1 40 62 70 61
girafeparis.com/en

Perruche

✱ Nicknamed the "high-altitude garden" because of its terrace location on the top floor of the department store Printemps, this is a practical stop after a day of shopping. It's open every day from 9:35 a.m. to 2 a.m., which leaves you plenty of opportunity to admire the Iron Lady—from afar, of course, but there she is, blending into the Paris skyline. The food is simple, but everything on the menu is tempting.

Printemps de l'Homme, 9th floor
2, rue du Havre, 9ᵉ
Tel. +33 (0)1 42 82 60 00
perruche.paris

Very trendy

Le Piaf

✳ If you want to be sure a dinner party will gel, this is the place to go. Get there at 8 p.m., chat with your friends a bit, order dinner (French classics revisited), and before you know it, you'll be singing at the top of your lungs with your friends and the piano man, as he bangs out songs everyone knows by heart. It's sure to be an evening you won't forget. I'm reminded of those wild nights out in Paris before I had kids … or a job (it's open until 5 a.m., Thursday to Saturday)!

38, rue Jean-Mermoz, 8e
Tel. +33 (0)1 47 42 64 10
lepiaf-paris.com

Clover Grill

✳ When you want a good piece of meat grilled to perfection, you know Jean-François Piège has the recipe. His style of cooking is in its element here, in generous servings of excellent products. But these are subtle flavors. The restaurant's friendly atmosphere shines through right down to the decorative wallpaper. This is the perfect place to bring a beau who likes quality meat (you might make an offhand remark like, "I think they have Australian Black Market beef").

6, rue Bailleul, 1er
Tel. +33 (0)1 40 41 59 59
clover-grill.com

CoCo

✳ I'm particularly fond of this first name, but the restaurant is also worth a visit because it's attached to the Opéra Garnier. The scene is set, not to mention the exceptional decor. You'll think you've walked into *The Great Gatsby*. (The interiors are by Corinne Sachot and florist Thierry Boutemy.) In good weather, the garden terrace within the Opéra is superb. The food is wonderfully prepared for a mouthwatering result. Don't miss the chocolate churros.

1, place Jacques-Rouché, 9ᵉ
Tel. +33 (0)1 42 68 86 80
coco-paris.com

Marigny, le Restaurant

✳ Located within the Théâtre Marigny, this is the perfect place for dinner before or after a show. It's also where to go when you feel like being a tourist on the Champs-Élysées. The Marigny is a star in the Jean-Louis Costes galaxy of restaurants, which are known for their luxe brasserie style and quality menus—there's something for everyone. This one is open daily from 9 a.m. to 2 a.m.

10 bis, avenue des Champs-Élysées, 8ᵉ
Tel. +33 (0)1 86 64 06 40
theatremarigny.fr

La Société

✳ Apparently this restaurant doesn't like to be included in guides. That's too bad, because it already featured in my first book and I also selected it for *The Parisian Field Guide to Men's Style*. I mention it again because it's well situated (across from the Saint-Germain church) and never disappoints.

4, place Saint-Germain-des-Prés, 6ᵉ
Tel. +33 (0)1 53 63 60 60

In a garden

La Table du Luxembourg and La Terrasse de Madame

It may not be obvious, but there's a wonderful place to have lunch in the Luxembourg Gardens: La Table du Luxembourg, in the shade of the most beautiful trees in Paris, next to the famous Théâtre des Marionnettes. You can hear birds singing and children playing—it feels like you're on vacation. It's a welcome break from routine and the food is tasty. Reservations are highly recommended, and you can make them online. There's another restaurant in the garden called La Terrasse de Madame that's also good. If you don't have time for a sit-down meal, you can order takeaway at the bar.

7, rue Guynemer, 6ᵉ
Tel. +33 (0)1 42 38 64 88
latableduluxembourg.com
218, rue de Médicis, 6ᵉ
Tel. +33 (0)1 42 01 17 96

Loulou

For a long time, the Tuileries Garden didn't have a restaurant worth going to, even for a snack. Everything changed with the opening of Loulou, the restaurant inside the Musée des Arts Décoratifs, whose wonderful terrace offers views of the Louvre. The food is simple and modern (seared tuna, parmesan artichokes). The crowd is a happy mix of tourists and Parisians. I like this place; it makes you feel cultivated because you can say, "I'm going to lunch at the Musée des Arts Décoratifs," which squashes any suspicion that you could've eaten at a fast-food joint.

107, rue de Rivoli, 1ᵉʳ
Tel. +33 (0)1 42 60 41 96
loulou-paris.com/welcome

Style and taste

A while back, my friend Héloïse (I worked with her years ago) started a subscription box that was so popular, she ran out within days. A fan of cooking, she created a website (missmaggieskitchen.com) where she sells charming kitchen objects and food, as well as little booklets with beautifully illustrated recipes. Héloïse is talented, beautiful, and generous. In fact she donates a portion of the profits to Action Against Hunger. But don't think I'm mentioning her because we have the same editor (keep an eye out for her forthcoming book); Flammarion just happens to choose incredible authors.

Bread & Roses

There was a Bread & Roses in the 6e *arrondissement* (7 rue de Fleurus), so obviously when this one opened in 2010 near my office, it became my new go-to lunch spot—and it still is. At lunch, the quiche, goat cheese on toast, tomato and mozzarella puff pastry tarts, and salads are excellent. The grain-filled organic bread is divine. And don't get me started on the pastries (Mont-Blanc, cheesecake, mille-feuilles). If you feel like a bit of organic bread at home or at the office, you can buy some at the back of the restaurant. Blissfully organic!

25, rue Boissy-d'Anglas, 8e
Tel. +33 (0)1 47 42 40 00
breadandroses.fr

Café Citron

A dinner under the lemon trees is what's in store at this restaurant created by designer Simon Porte Jacquemus and Kaspia. Located on the Champ-Élysées, in the new Galeries Lafayette building, if offers sunny fare. From the tableware to the straw rugs to the menu, the designer infused everything with his native Provence. Not only do I love what he does, but I love the feeling of dining in the South without having to leave Paris.

Galeries Lafayette Champs-Élysées
60, avenue des Champs-Élysées, 8ᵉ
Tel. +33 (0)1 83 65 61 08
cafecitronparis.com

GASTRONOMIC FOOD HALL

If you're looking for a chic food hall where you can have lunch or dinner made with high-quality products, head to Beaupassage (53–57, rue de Grenelle, 7ᵉ). You'll find only the best in fine dining by the masters: Thierry Marx, Yannick Alléno, Anne-Sophie Pic, Pierre Hermé, along with the cheese shop Barthélémy. A special tip of the hat to Alexandre Polmard, breeder-butcher, whose restaurant is very "stable chic."

Ralph's

✳ Ralph Lauren was right to choose the Left Bank for his largest European store. This seventeenth-century *hôtel particulier* is entirely dedicated to the creations of the American king of sportswear style. The highlight? The shady courtyard of Ralph's restaurant. Crabcake or burger? You may be in Paris, but you'll be eating American. I've said it before: the *Parisienne* likes to mix it up.

173, boulevard Saint-Germain, 6ᵉ
Tel. +33 (0)1 44 77 76 00
ralphlauren.com

An app for foodies

If you're still hungry, despite all the restaurants I've recommended, there's an app you must download: Le Fooding, an inventory of the best tables in the city (and the nicest, which are always affordable). Le Fooding puts out a ranking that Parisians all know by heart.
lefooding.fr/en

Claus

✳ The owner of this restaurant, known for its wonderful breakfasts, used to work in fashion. The lunches are very good, too—and very healthy. The atmosphere is pleasant, but be warned, there's often a line.

2, rue Clément, 6ᵉ
14, rue Jean-Jacques Rousseau, 1ᵉʳ
Tel. +33 (0)1 55 26 95 10
clausparis.com

Le Drugstore

✳ The designer Tom Dixon took classic brasserie decor and turned it on its head. Chef Eric Frechon runs the menu at this restaurant, where everyone is up by 8 a.m. to start preparations. Try the legendary *Parisien*, a ham-and-butter sandwich. Service runs non-stop, noon to midnight. That's also very Paris!

133, avenue des Champs-Élysées, 8ᵉ
Tel. +33 (0)1 44 43 75 07
publicisdrugstore.com/en

BONNE NUIT!

Where should you sleep in Paris?
The luxury hotels are always a good solution—
a stay at the Ritz or the Crillon rarely disappoints.
But you have your pick of boutique hotels as well.
Good location (mostly on the Left Bank),
great decor, and lots of charm: here are my top
places to rest your head while in Paris.

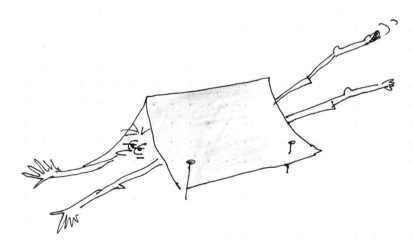

Hôtel National des Arts et Métiers

The atmosphere

✳ Despite a low-key appearance, this four-star establishment—located between the Marais and Montorgeuil—has an impressive terrace with a panoramic view of the capital. Stars are known to come here for happy hour.

CONCIERGE'S NOTE

"No, the Ristorante National inside the hotel isn't a formal restaurant, it's a chic trattoria."

The decor

✳ Environmentally friendly: this hotel places the accent on materials like cut stone, terrazzo, steel, and wood.

243, rue Saint-Martin, 3ᵉ
Tel. +33 (0)1 80 97 22 80
hotelnational.paris/en

Hotel Bel Ami

The atmosphere

✱ Design, design, design—but with a hint of softness. The concierge service is very good at organizing family tours of the city or trips to Versailles. And when you return exhausted from a day of wandering around, there's a spa and a sauna to relax in. As for the location, it's perfect if you like the Left Bank but want easy access to the Right Bank.

The decor

✱ Very contemporary and created by artists. Three of the four floors were renovated by the designer Pascal Allaman, who wanted to create a bold impression with references to calligraphy and the defunct printer that used to occupy the space.

CONCIERGE'S NOTE

"I hit the sauna before heading to Café de Flore."

From €373 (c. £340/$420)
7–11, rue Saint-Benoît, 6ᵉ
Tel. +33 (0)1 42 61 53 53
hotelbelami-paris.com

Hôtel Récamier

The atmosphere

✱ Wonderfully situated (next to Saint-Sulpice church), this hotel is one of the best-kept secrets in Paris (well, it *was* anyway!). Hidden away but located in a very popular area, it has the charm of not seeking fame at all costs. Plus, the staff is very welcoming.

The decor

✱ All the rooms are different. The interiors recently took a minimalist turn: beige dominates, with touches of dark colors that differ from room to room.

From €259 (c. £238/$289, check website for deals)
3 bis, place Saint-Sulpice, 6ᵉ
Tel. +33 (0)1 43 26 04 89
hotelrecamier.com

Villa Madame

The atmosphere

✱ Luxury without pretension: a low-profile address that's both contemporary and chic on a very charming street in the 6ᵉ *arrondissement*. The best part? The garden.

The decor

✱ Light wood, exotic decorative objects, beige, brown, white, and orchid—a basic combination but one that gives the design warmth. Ask for one of the rooms with a terrace and a view over the Paris skyline.

From €160 (c. £145/$175)
44, rue Madame, 6ᵉ
Tel. +33 (0)1 45 48 02 81
hotelvillamadameparis.com

Villa d'Estrées

The atmosphere

✳ While the hotel itself is good, the location is what really stands out. From here, you can explore both the Left and Right Banks. Room service runs until 11:30 p.m. and connected rooms can accommodate up to five people.

The decor

✳ Ultra-classic: simple colors that everyone likes. Some rooms have striped wallpaper, but it's all in very good taste.

From €170 (c. £155/$189)
17, rue Git-le-Coeur, 6ᵉ
Tel. +33 (0)1 55 42 71 11
villadestrees.com

Le Brach

The decor

✱ By Philippe Starck. Built in a 75,000-square-foot (7,000 m²) former postal sorting center from the 1970s, here 1930s architecture meets modernism, the Bauhaus, Dada, and the surrealists. Unusual objects and works of art make for a welcoming atmosphere.

CONCIERGE'S NOTE

"Go visit the chickens on the roof."

The atmosphere

✱ This is the only hotel in the area to have an edginess that you usually find in more central Paris hotels or in the city's eastern neighborhoods. It's new and proves that the 16ᵉ *arrondissement* has become very hip. Locals like to say that it's not a hotel, but a gathering place; there's even a kitchen garden on the roof with three egg-laying chickens.

From €437 (c. £400/$487)
1–7, rue Jean-Richepin, 16ᵉ
Tel. +33 (0)1 44 30 10 00
brachparis.com/?lang=en

L'Hôtel

The atmosphere

✱ You can tell right away this hotel has a story. It was part of French Renaissance Queen Margot's residence. Following a recent remodel, it has become a favorite with the fashion set. Don't miss the restaurant, called simply Le Restaurant, or the pool, located under the arches and reserved for guests.

The decor

✱ By Jacques Garcia: think red velvet, antique furniture, gold lamps, illustrated wallpaper, and luxurious fabrics. It's all welcoming in a classic way. The terrace in the largest suite looks out over the rooftops of Paris. Incredible.

CONCIERGE'S NOTE

"Arty, intellectual, glam, and rock-and-roll—everyone likes this hotel!"

From €320 (c. £285/$357)
13, rue des Beaux-Arts, 6ᵉ
Tel. +33 (0)1 44 41 99 00
l-hotel.com

Hôtel de l'Abbaye Saint-Germain

The atmosphere

✳ Very calm; it's one of the few refined classics that isn't overpriced. Located in Saint-Germain-des-Prés, it's popular with fashionistas who like being able to stop by the hotel to drop off their bags. In summer, you can have breakfast in the shady courtyard to the sound of the bubbling fountain— a highlight of the hotel!

The decor

✳ Flowery or striped wallpaper, large gilded mirrors, matching headboards and lampshades, marble bathrooms: this is one-hundred-percent refined classic.

From €245 (c. £225/$275)
10, rue Cassette, 6ᵉ
Tel. +33 (0)1 45 44 38 11
hotelabbayeparis.com

CONCIERGE'S NOTE

"There used to be a chapel and a convent where the hotel now stands, so of course it's calm."

CONCIERGE'S NOTE

"I'm not coming to the museum with you— I'm going to the pool."

Hôtel Paris Bastille Boutet

The atmosphere

✳ This lovely five-star hotel near Bastille took over a historical location in a chocolate factory and crafted an identity around leafy terraces.

The decor

✳ White and wood—obviously my kind of thing!

From €200 (c. £185/$225)
22–24, rue Faidherbe, 11ᵉ
Tel. +33 (0)1 40 24 65 65
hotel-paris-bastille-boutet.com/en

Ines thanks...

My coauthor and very dear friend Sophie, worn out from working so hard (I'm doing fine, which probably tells you which of us had to do the most work on this edition), suggested we thank our readers. Personally, I hope they'll be thanking us!

But I don't want to seem entirely ungrateful, so:

✳ Thanks to our editor, Julie Rouart, whom we've known since preadolescence (a long time, anyway) and who continues to support us, in the English sense of the word as well as the French (i.e. put up with us!)

✳ Thanks to the maître d's who don't say *Bonne dégustation!*

✳ Thanks to the translator of this book, especially for the preceding phrase, which doesn't mean anything in Polish, Portuguese, Italian, or modern Greek.

✳ Thanks to those who caught on that this book has been published in many languages.

✳ Thanks to Denis Olivennes, an extraordinary man. Thanks to those who know I'm not joking.

✳ Thanks to Stanislas, Sophie's love, because apparently he's extraordinary, too.

✳ Thanks, Zohra, for preparing fresh carrot juice for us so I could photograph it. (What's that plastic straw doing there?! Whale killers! Well, it looked nice in the photo.)

✳ Thanks, Nine, for believing me ten years ago when I said there wasn't a budget for a model for this book, and for accepting to pose. Actually, my publisher is loaded, but I wanted my baby girl in there!

✳ Thanks, Violette, for continuing to steal clothes from your mother: it proves I still have good taste.

✳ Thanks, Sienna. You are so pretty that one day you'll be posing for this book, so let's get off on the right foot. It was so nice of you to drop off that Swiss cream I love so much. Like daughter, like coauthor! Kiss Aramis and Vadim for me.

✳ Thanks, Benjamin, for reading everything and for even getting as far as this!

✳ Thanks, Diego Della Valle, my wonderful boss at Roger Vivier, who finds everything I do amusing. Please note: always thank your boss, even if it seems off topic.

✱ Thank you, Simon, for showing up in a tank top while Sophie and I were making corrections on good taste. Argghhh—you'll be president one day and then we won't be able to make fun of you anymore.

✱ Paul, I'm preparing a book especially for you and your suits, just to annoy Nathan, so I'm not going to mention you in the acknowledgments right now, ok?

✱ Thanks to Tiphaine, who understood straight away that design would be essential to this book. Hey, I can be serious sometimes, too, can't I?

✱ Thanks to Yann Barthes, for inviting us on his show, *Quotidien*. (Sophie, ask our editor if we can make personalized books for journalists with their name, you know, like those books for kids!)

✱ Thank you for the *ELLE* cover announcing the publication of our new, revamped book and for letting me keep my clothes on!

✱ Thank you, Frédéric Périgot. (You have nothing to do with this book, but I like you.)

✱ Thank you to the kind bookstore owner who does so much for us. (They know who they are.)

✱ Thanks, Kevin. (Lawyers like to read.)

✱ Thank you, Jeanne and Émilion, for bringing the wet towels back from the pool. Thanks, Sophie, for giving the preceding, surreal sentence a pass. I promise, no one will notice.

✱ Thank you to the readers of lalettredines.fr who, in addition to this book, never get tired of receiving addresses and advice in their inbox each week. #self-publicity.

✱ Thank you, my dear Gachet. Without you, I would NEVER have written this book. You think of everything, you know me better than I know myself, and it's been a real pleasure working on it with you. Ok, you can't take out that last sentence, otherwise I'll tell everyone that you almost always dress in black!

✱ Thank you, France! Ok, that may be a little pompous, but it's clear, right?

Photo Credits

All photographs are copyright © the brands and businesses, with the exception of the following:

© Abaca Corporate/Didier Delmas: p. 237
© Pierre Antoine/Musée Cognacq-Jay:
    p. 192 (top)
© A.P.C.: pp. 69 (bottom, center), 99
© Sophie Arancio: p. 142 (top)
© BA&SH: p. 85
© Christian Baraja: p. 191
© Bella Jones: p. 88
© Alain Beulé: p. 142 (bottom)
© Christophe Bielsa: p. 234
© Bijoux Monic Paris: p. 110
© Bonpoint: p. 195
© Dimitri Coste: p. 107
© Alban Couturier: p. 195
© Culturespaces/Sofiacome: p. 190
© Adrien Dirand: p. 223 (top)
© Mélanie Elbaz: p. 89
© Zo Fan: p. 104
© Flammarion/photo: Rodolphe Bricard:
    pp. 66 (middle, left and bottom, center),
    71 (bottom, left), 73–77
© Alexis Flandrin: p. 95 (right)
© Ines de la Fressange: p. 167 (top)
© Ines de la Fressange and Sophie Gachet:
    pp. 69 (top, right and bottom, left), 71 (bottom,
    center), 215, 227
© Ines de la Fressange Paris: p. 69 (top, right and
    bottom, left)
© Sophie Gachet: pp. 71 (top, left and right),
    79, 148–55, 157, 159–63, 165, 167 (bottom),
    168, 198
© Virginie Garnier: p. 217
© Constance Gennari/The Socialite Family:
    p. 172
© Thomas Gizolme: p. 106
© Hervé Goluza: pp. 143, 209 (top, left and right)
© Julien M. Hekimian/GETTY IMAGES
    EUROPE/Getty Images/AFP: p. 24 (right)
© JACQUEMUS: p. 228
© JCR Paris: p. 84
© K. Jacques: p. 66 (top, center)
© Stephen Kent Johnson: p. 175
© Franziska Krug/Getty Images for Roger
    Vivier: p. 24 (left)
© Pierrelouis Lacombe: p. 108
© Le Bon Marché: p. 98
© Max Ledieu: p. 211
© Benoît Linero: p. 218
© Nicolas Lobbestael: p. 224 (bottom)

© Frédéric Lucano: p. 103
© Pierre Lucet-Penato: p. 139
© Maison de Vacances /Olivier Fritze: p. 173
© Maison Guerlain/Philippe Garcia: p. 141
© Dominique Maître: p. 86
© Pierre Mansiet : p. 97
© Marc McCourt: p. 96
© Mr. Tripper (Patrick Locqueneux): p. 214
© Amy Murrell: p. 236
© Musée du Louvre/Olivier Ouadah 2017:
    p. 192 (bottom)
© Alexis Narodetzky: p. 232
© Denis Olivennes: p. 164
© Palais de Tokyo, 2019/photo: Aurélie Cenno:
    pp. 196–97
© Tommy Pascal: p. 140 (bottom)
© Jean-Baptiste Pellerin: p. 116
© Benoît Peverelli: pp. 17–23, 53–55, 57, 59–60,
    63, 65, 68, 70
© Marc Piasecki/GC Images: p. 25 (left)
© Présidence de la République: p. 187
© Mathieu Rainaud: p. 226
© Romain Ricard: pp. 223 (bottom), 224 (top),
    225
© Bertrand Rinhoff: p. 181 (bottom)
© Thibaud Robic: p. 87
© Samuel de Roman/GETTY IMAGES
    EUROPE/Getty Images/AFP: p. 25 (right)
© Matthieu Salvaing: pp. 115 (top, left, and
    bottom), 222
© Marcelle Senmêle: p. 200 (bottom)
© Sandra Serraf: p. 90
© E. Sicot: p. 144
© The Guild of Saint Luke Company: p. 221
© Tomiko Taira: p. 184
© Marie-Amélie Tondu: p. 145 (top)
© Uniiti: pp. 216, 220
© Univers Presse: pp. 92, 109
© Roberta Valerio: p. 102
© Julien Vallé: p. 91
© Cornelis Van Voorthuizen: p. 95 (left)
© Roger Vivier: pp. 66 (middle, right), 69 (top,
    left and bottom, right), 105
© Alexander Volodin: p. 235

All rights reserved: pp. 66 (top, left and right and
bottom, left and right), 178, 207, 212–13, 219